Babylonia: A Very Short Introduction

VERY SHORT INTRODUCTIONS are for anyone wanting a stimulating and accessible way into a new subject. They are written by experts, and have been translated into more than 45 different languages.

The series began in 1995, and now covers a wide variety of topics in every discipline. The VSI library now contains over 500 volumes—a Very Short Introduction to everything from Psychology and Philosophy of Science to American History and Relativity—and continues to grow in every subject area.

Titles in the series include the following:

Trevor Bryce

BABYLONIA

A Very Short Introduction

UNIVERSITY PRESS

Great Clarendon Street, Oxford, OX2 6DP,
United Kingdom

Oxford University Press is a department of the University of Oxford.
It furthers the University's objective of excellence in research, scholarship,
and education by publishing worldwide. Oxford is a registered trade mark of
Oxford University Press in the UK and in certain other countries

Published in the United States of America by Oxford University Press
198 Madison Avenue, New York, NY 10016, United States of America

British Library Cataloguing in Publication Data
Data available

Library of Congress Control Number: 2016934338

ISBN 978-0-19-872647-0

Printed and bound by
CPI Group (UK) Ltd, Croydon, CR0 4YY

Contents

Babylonia

Acknowledgements

It has been a pleasure to work with OUP's editorial staff, particularly Andrea Keegan, Jenny Nugee, and Carrie Hickman, throughout this project. My sincere thanks are due also to the School of Historical and Philosophical Inquiry, University of Queensland, for its valuable infrastructural support. I am most grateful to Dr Heather Baker, who read the manuscript in draft and suggested many valuable improvements, and to OUP's anonymous external reviewer, from whose comments I have gained much benefit in preparing the final manuscript of this book. Once again, I wish to express my sincere thanks to Dorothy McCarthy, who has copy-edited two of my previous books, for her careful reading of the text and her meticulous attention to detail in preparing this book for publication.

Trevor Bryce, University of Queensland

September, 2015

List of illustrations

Introduction

Babylon was one of the greatest cities of the ancient world (Figure 1). Its very name, like that of Rome, evokes an image of power, wealth, and splendour—and decadence. The two names are closely linked in biblical tradition, for in the Book of Revelation Rome is damned as the 'Whore of Babylon'—and thus identified with a city whose image of oppression and wantonness persisted and flourished long after the city itself had crumbled into piles of dust. We shall see how Babylon's biblical image has in so many respects been countered by the recovery of its own history and civilization, through the decipherment of the language of its tablets and the sifting of its archaeological remains. Both sets of sources reveal to us a city whose origins date back almost two thousand years before the foundation of Rome. Among the longest continuously inhabited urban settlements in human history, it became the centre of one of the most culturally and intellectually vibrant civilizations of the ancient world, exercising a profound influence on its Near Eastern contemporaries, and contributing in many respects to the religious, scientific, and literary traditions of the Classical world.

However, the pages that follow deal not just with Babylon, but with the whole of southern Mesopotamia, extending southwards from modern Baghdad, in the region where the Tigris and the Euphrates closely approach each other, through the marshlands

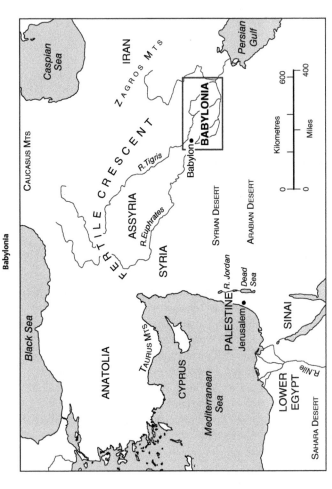

1. The ancient Near Eastern world.

in the deep south to the Persian Gulf. Babylon, lying on the Euphrates just south-west of Baghdad, was but one of many urban communities that arose in southern Mesopotamia during the third millennium BC, the period we call the Early Bronze Age. By the time the small village that was to become the city of biblical notoriety had been born, probably around the middle of the millennium, southern Mesopotamia had for centuries been the homeland of a cluster of city-states which made up the Sumerian civilization. Commonly referred to as 'the cradle of civilization', the land we call Sumer (its own inhabitants called it Kengir) emerged early in the millennium as the first major focus of organized urban life in the Near East.

There is still debate over the origins of the Sumerians—whether they were newcomers arriving in Mesopotamia at the end of the fourth millennium, or whether they evolved out of the indigenous peoples of the region. In any case, their high level of practical and organizational skills enabled them to master the harsh natural environment in which they lived, and to thrive, not merely survive, in it. Large desert tracts occupied much of the flat, mostly arid plain that lay between the Tigris and Euphrates, barely moistened by the region's meagre rainfall which frequently failed altogether. Drought was an ever-present threat to human survival.

The Sumerians confronted the threat and triumphed over it. Their building of a large network of canals which formed a complex irrigation system was one of their outstanding practical achievements. It was this achievement above all that enabled them to turn a region so hostile to human development into the homeland of a prosperous, sophisticated civilization. The era of the Sumerian city-states is known as the Early Dynastic period, generally dated from *c.*2900 to 2334 BC. It was an era of great material prosperity, due both to the Sumerians' effective exploitation of the natural environment and to their extensive trading enterprises. (The latter were necessitated by the almost total lack of natural resources in the region, like timber and metals.)

It was also an era of outstanding artistic achievement—illustrated by the famous artworks produced by Sumerians artists and craftsmen, like those from the so-called royal tombs of Ur.

The end of the Early Dynastic period came with the rise of a new power in the northern part of southern Mesopotamia. Through much if not all of the Sumerian period, southern Mesopotamia was inhabited by another ethnic group, this one of Semitic origin. Derived from the name Shem, one of Noah's sons, 'Semite' (adjective 'Semitic') is a term coined in the eighteenth century AD to refer to a number of prominent western Asian population groups, including the Babylonians, Assyrians, Canaanites, Phoenicians, Hebrews, and Arabs, because of certain similarities observable in their languages and cultures. Around 2334, a Semitic leader called Sargon founded a ruling dynasty in the city Agade (location as yet unknown) in the northern part of southern Mesopotamia, and established the first empire in Near Eastern history. Called the Akkadian empire, it extended at the height of its power over the whole of Mesopotamia, as far north as Kurdistan, east to the Zagros mountains, and as far west as south-eastern Anatolia (though we cannot be sure how much direct control the Akkadians actually exercised through all these regions).

Various factors contributed to its fall *c*.2193. But within a century another empire arose, this one based on the city of Ur, which lay in the southernmost part of Mesopotamia. Founded by Ur-Namma *c*.2112, the empire of what is called the Ur III dynasty encompassed the whole of southern Mesopotamia and included substantial subject territories east of the Tigris. But it was even shorter-lived than its Akkadian predecessor. Around 2004, it was destroyed by Elamite invaders from western Iran.

Babylon played no significant role in this Early Bronze Age saga. Indeed, the first reference to it in written records does not occur until *c*.2200, in the period of the Akkadian empire. By this time, the city had at least two temples, and it subsequently became a provincial administrative centre of the Ur III empire. But the real beginning of its rise to importance was still some 150 years away. Around the year 1880, a man called Sumu-la-El established a royal dynasty in the city. Under the fifth king of this dynasty, Hammurabi (Hammurapi), Babylon became the centre of a major Near Eastern kingdom, the first of several such kingdoms in its long history.

We shall be looking closely at Hammurabi's reign (1792–1750) in the following chapters. But let us first say something about the names 'Babylon' and 'Babylonia'. In the Akkadian period, Babylon was called *Bāb-ilim*—'Gate of God'. *Ka-dingirra*, the city's Sumerian name, has the same meaning. We don't know which name was earlier, but it was the Akkadian one that became firmly established in ancient tradition. From it was derived the Greek name for the city, 'Babylon'. In Hebrew the city was called *Bābel*.

Self-evidently derived from 'Babylon', 'Babylonia' is not an ancient name. It's one adopted by modern scholars to refer to southern Mesopotamia from the first time it was dominated by the city of Babylon, particularly from Hammurabi's reign onwards. Some scholars, however, say that the term should not really be used until the period when a Kassite dynasty held sway over the region—in the Late Bronze Age; it was only then that 'Babylonia' became a coherent geopolitical unit, and largely remained that way for the rest of its ancient history, even when it was subject to other powers, like Assyria, Persia, and Rome. Nevertheless, Hammurabi's dynasty, and more especially Hammurabi's own reign, marks a convenient starting-point for our journey across the eras through which the history of southern Mesopotamia—'Babylonia'—passed.

Our journey will take us from the Old Babylonian kingdom of Hammurabi through the period of the second great Babylonian kingdom, ruled by the Kassites, and then through a long period of relative insignificance until Babylon shines forth more splendidly than ever as the capital of the Neo-Babylonian empire. This was when Nebuchadnezzar II (604–562) became the Near Eastern world's most powerful king. From there our journey will take us through the periods of Persian and Macedonian rule, the latter ending with Alexander the Great's death in Babylon in 323 BC. In the following Hellenistic Age, Babylonia was absorbed into the Seleucid empire. Finally, we shall proceed to the Roman imperial period when Babylon became little more than a derelict ruin. That is how it was when the Roman emperor Trajan visited its site in the early second century AD, to pay homage to Alexander's memory.

Chapter 1
The Old Babylonian period:
(c.1880–1595 BC)

Peoples and kingdoms of the early
second millennium

Hammurabi's dynasty, and indeed most of the inhabitants of
Babylon and other Babylonian cities at the time, belonged to one
of the most powerful and widespread ethnic groups in the Near
East. They were called the Amorites. Their name is best known
to us from its appearance in the Old Testament List of Nations
(e.g. Deut. 20: 16–17), though the 'biblical Amorites' may have
been only indirectly connected with the peoples so designated in
earlier historical sources. Speaking a Semitic language, the
Amorites were originally nomadic groups, inhabiting large parts
of Syria and Palestine, who gradually spread eastwards across
the Euphrates into southern Mesopotamia as they sought new
pastures for their flocks and herds. Some of these groups
maintained their traditional nomadic lifestyle for centuries to
come, but others quickly adopted a more settled way of life
when they moved into urban centres, as we know from texts
found in the city of Ebla in northern Syria, dating to the
twenty-fourth century BC. (Throughout this book, we shall
use the term 'Syria' in its ancient context to refer to the
regions lying between the Euphrates and the eastern
Mediterranean coast.)

In the early centuries of the second millennium, Amorite leaders began to establish major kingdoms of their own in Mesopotamia and Syria, after the fall of the first great Near Eastern kingdoms in the previous millennium. Notable among the new players was the Kingdom of Upper Mesopotamia, established by an Amorite ruler called Samsi-Addu (Akkadian Shamshi-Adad) in the early eighteenth century. The traditional capital of the region was the city of Ashur on the Tigris river. Samsi-Addu also established viceregal seats at Ekallatum, probably on the Tigris not far from Ashur (its exact location is unknown), and at Mari on the west bank of the middle Euphrates. This period also saw the rise of other kingdoms established by Amorite dynasties. They included, in Syria, the kingdom of Yamhad, founded by an Amorite leader called Sumu-epuh, who ruled from his capital Aleppo, and further south, just east of the Orontes river, the kingdom of Qatna.

Further ingredients in the political brew of kingdoms to become prominent in Syria and Mesopotamia during this period were three located in southern Mesopotamia. Isin and Larsa, the earliest of these, became bitter rivals in their attempts to fill the power vacuum left by the fall of the Ur III empire. After a long series of conflicts between them, Larsa emerged victorious under its king Rim-Sin who incorporated his defeated rival's kingdom into his own c.1794. The conqueror enjoyed supremacy in the region for some three decades. But he was finally overthrown and his kingdom seized by his powerful neighbour, Hammurabi, king of Babylon (c.1763).

Hammurabi and his dynastic predecessors

Hammurabi's reign marked the peak period in his dynasty's tenure of power in the Near East, particularly in the middle Euphrates region and southern Mesopotamia (Figure 2). In Babylonian tradition, a nomadic Amorite chieftain called Sumu-abum (c.1894–1881) is considered to be the founder of the royal dynasty to which Hammurabi belonged. Sumu-abum was highly regarded

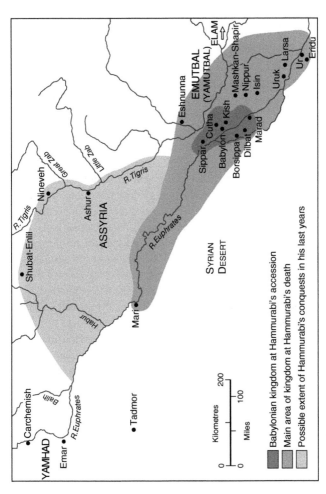

2. **The kingdom of Hammurabi.**

in his own time, and revered in later times. And he may well have brought to pre-eminence the Amorite group that subsequently established the kingdom of Babylon. But since he himself never took up residence in Babylon, scholars now prefer to regard a man called Sumu-la-El (*c.*1880–1845), who succeeded him, as the real founder of the kingdom. Sumu-la-El is credited with building a royal palace and a great fortification wall around the city. Other early Babylonian kings oversaw the construction of new canals within it. However, the most significant canals built by the Old Babylonian rulers were located in the agricultural countryside. These waterways were Babylonia's life-blood, providing an essential basis for the country's future growth and prosperity.

But Babylon still remained a relatively insignificant player in the Near Eastern world during the time-span of almost nine decades extending from Sumu-la-El's accession to the death of his third successor, Hammurabi's father Sin-muballit *c.*1793. Isin and Larsa were the major powers in southern Mesopotamia during this time, and Eshnunna in the Diyala river basin and Elam in south-western Iran were emerging as other great powers of the age. But despite the constant threat all of them posed to the Babylonian kingdom's very existence, the relatively small land ruled by Sin-muballit (probably less than 10,000 square kilometres) was in pretty good shape when Hammurabi inherited it from him. It was internally stable, relatively prosperous, and reasonably secure from outside attack because of its strongly fortified cities.

Even so, its existence remained tenuous. Survival in this age meant forming alliances with (and sometimes even accepting submission to) the stronger powers of the region. For Babylon these were Samsi-Addu's Kingdom of Upper Mesopotamia in the north and the kingdom of Larsa, then ruled by Rim-Sin, in the south. Judicious political and military alliances with his powerful neighbours, which kept them on side and secured their protection against other powers of the age, gave Hammurabi sufficient breathing space to build on the economic foundations established by his father, with further work on canal construction, and to strengthen his capital's fortifications. This he coupled with the maintenance of existing temples and the building of new ones. His support of the kingdom's scribal centres must have helped boost the kingdom's administrative efficiency, and this together with a programme of social reforms further enhanced the kingdom's internal stability. In his building and judicial activities in particular, Hammurabi demonstrated two of the most important responsibilities of a king—that of a great builder and a great social reformer.

Perhaps already at the beginning of his reign, Hammurabi had a vision of becoming a great military leader as well. The protection and consolidation of what he already had would be given first priority. But already in the sixth year of his reign, he gave notice of his expansionist ambitions, flexing his military muscles to raid Isin and Uruk, which then belonged to the kingdom of Larsa, and conducting further campaigns in the next few years against other states in his region. By the middle of his reign, Hammurabi had clearly emerged as one of the significant rulers of the age. This is made explicit in a letter written by a court official at Mari, then ruled by a man called Zimri-Lim, to some of the king's vassal subjects. Part of it reads: *No king wields power just by himself. Ten to fifteen kings follow Hammurabi of Babylon, the same number follow Rim-Sin of Larsa, Ibal-pi-El of Eshnunna and Amut-pi-El of Qatna, and twenty kings follow Yarim-Lim of Yamhad.*

To this list of five kingdoms, we should add Mari, as the official does later in the document, and to the east the kingdom of Elam, whose current ruler was probably the most powerful of them all. Between them, the overlords of these lands controlled a vast expanse of territory extending from western Syria through Mesopotamia and south-western Iran. The fact that aggression by one of them against another was likely to trigger coalitions of the rest against him was a reasonably effective guarantee of relative peace and stability throughout the region. Eventually, after forming a series of astute alliances with one or other of his foreign peers, Hammurabi was ready to turn from largely defensive strategies to more aggressive expansionist campaigns of his own. This turning point in his reign came in the year 1763, three decades after his accession.

In this year, he confronted a coalition led by the Elamites which included troops from Eshnunna, and defeated it, giving him control of a significant swathe of territory in the Tigris region. The following year Eshnunna itself fell to him. Around this time too, he directed his military might against Larsa, on the pretext that it had refused him support in his war against the Elamites, and captured it after a six-month siege. Thus ended the long reign of Larsa's most distinguished ruler Rim-Sin, who became Hammurabi's prisoner. Hammurabi spared the city itself, its inhabitants and its buildings, demolishing only its fortifications. Larsa thus became an integral part of the rapidly expanding Babylonian kingdom, and along with it all Larsa's subject territories, including Isin, Ur, and Uruk. But Hammurabi was not yet done.

He now turned his attention west of the Euphrates, marching into the kingdom of Mari and occupying its capital. For several months he and his troops remained there, long enough to loot it of most of its contents for transport back to Babylon. Then he torched all its monumental buildings. The only significant states that now retained their independence from Babylon were the western Syrian kingdoms Yamhad (Aleppo) and Qatna. Their remoteness from Hammurabi's power-base secured them against any serious threat of a Babylonian invasion.

In his final years, Hammurabi appears to have conducted at least two campaigns into northern Mesopotamia. These would have taken his armies through most of the northern territories of the former Kingdom of Upper Mesopotamia. Though he may not have won any significant measure of control over them, his military achievements in his last decade upon the throne had undoubtedly made him the most powerful king in Mesopotamia. Indeed he boasted that he was 'the king who made obedient the four quarters of the earth'. His claim was clearly an exaggerated one. But at that time he was equalled in political and military might only by the ruler of Yamhad who controlled much of the region between the Euphrates and the Mediterranean Sea. Babylon and Yamhad now shared undisputed dominance of the Near Eastern world.

Hammurabi's successors

Under his five successors, all of whom had long reigns, the kingdom built by Hammurabi was to last another 155 years. But within a few years of the great man's death, decline had set in. This was evident in the reign of his son and successor Samsu-iluna (c.1749–1712) who had already assumed some of the responsibilities of kingship in Hammurabi's last years. Samsu-iluna seems to have been a conscientious and vigorous ruler who tried to maintain the status and power his father had won for the kingdom, and perhaps even to build upon it. Thus he may have campaigned along the Euphrates beyond Mari and succeeded in annexing, temporarily, the territory of a newly developing kingdom there called Hana; its ruler had sought to fill the power vacuum in the region left by the fall of Mari.

But elsewhere in the Babylonian kingdom, particularly in its southern half, serious problems had emerged by the tenth year of Samsu-iluna's reign. Texts from his tenth and eleventh years indicate that the king had lost control of a number of his southern cities (environmental as well as political reasons have been suggested as the reasons for this), including, probably, the holy city of Nippur. So too the city of Ur in the far south. The northern part of Babylonia seems to have remained stable and prosperous

13

under Samsu-iluna's stewardship, and indeed its cities may have provided new homes for refugees from the southern Babylonian cities. But political volatility continued in the south, with uprisings there as well as in the north-eastern and eastern border regions. These probably continued for the rest of Samsu-iluna's reign, and indeed well beyond it.

They were caused, or at least given added force, by the appearance of new tribal elements in Babylonia. Notable among these was a group of horse-breeding immigrants from the east who initially occupied parts of the Tigris region before spreading across Babylonia to the middle Euphrates. Their infiltration into Babylonia seems by and large to have been a peaceful one; they appear in the texts as mercenaries and as hired labourers on agricultural estates, and sometimes as purchasers of property of their own. But they were also involved in confrontations with the Babylonians, as indicated in texts from the reigns of Samsu-iluna and his son and successor Abi-eshuh. They were called the Kassites.

In his final years on the throne, Samsu-iluna was faced with another serious threat—this time from the marshlands in the far south of Babylonia. Here arose a new power called the First Sealand Dynasty. The Sealanders added much to the disruptions in southern Babylonia during Samsu-iluna's and Abi-eshuh's reigns. They may for a time have controlled parts of northern Babylonian territory as well.

Like their predecessors, the last three kings of the Old Babylonian dynasty seem to have applied themselves diligently to the responsibilities of kingship—building and maintaining canal systems, strengthening the fortifications of the cities under their control, and putting down rebellions. None succeeded in reversing the decline of the Babylonian kingdom. But they did maintain control of the territories and cities of northern Babylonia. And thanks to their active promotion and encouragement, science, including mathematics, and the arts in general appear to have had a relatively flourishing existence in the cities still under their control. This is reflected in the establishment of a number of scribal centres, with royal support. They fulfilled their religious obligations by building or repairing temples and sanctuaries, especially to honour the god Marduk, in Babylon and other cities. And they conscientiously maintained their roles as guardians of justice, as illustrated by their practice of issuing *mīšarum* decrees throughout their reigns, decrees concerned particularly with reforms designed to provide relief for those suffering from unrepayable debt burdens.

The final episode in the history of the Old Babylonian kingdom dates to the beginning of the sixteenth century. Around the year 1595, Mursili I, king of the Hittites, followed up his triumphant campaign in northern Syria, which ended with his destruction of the kingdom of Aleppo, by marching east to the Euphrates then south along it to Babylon. This was during the reign of Samsu-ditana, the last of Hammurabi's dynastic successors. Mursili laid siege to the royal capital, conquered, plundered, and destroyed it. The Old Babylonian Kingdom was at an end.

Chapter 2
Babylonian society through the perspective of Hammurabi's Laws

*So that the strong might not oppress the weak, to provide
justice for the orphan and the widow, I have engraved
my precious pronouncements upon my stele and erected it
before the statue of me, the king of justice, in Babylon, the
city raised high by the gods Anu and Enlil, within
Esangila, the temple whose foundations are firm like
heaven and earth, in order to give the judgements and
verdicts of the land, and to provide justice for the
oppressed.*

(From the Epilogue of the Laws of Hammurabi)

Hammurabi's stele

During their AD 1901–2 excavations of the ancient city of Susa,
located in south-western Iran and traditional capital of the
kingdom of Elam, French excavators unearthed an imposing
stele (pillar) some 2.2 metres high, carved from a black stone
called diorite (Figure 3). It was covered front and back with an
inscription, hundreds of lines in length. Surmounting the
inscription, and occupying the top third of the stele's front side,
was a depiction of a god seated on his throne, and a human figure
standing before him. The stele had been one of the most prized
trophies brought back to Susa by a twelfth-century Elamite king
from his campaigns of conquest and plunder in Mesopotamia.

3. Hammurabi and the god Shamash, Laws stele.

The deity depicted on the stele was Shamash, god of justice; the figure standing before him was his deputy on earth, the Babylonian king Hammurabi, in the act of receiving from his god the 'rod and ring', probably a measuring rod and a coiled length of rope—as symbols of rule.

The stele is inscribed with a series of laws which largely define Hammurabi's role as the Shepherd of his people, above all as the protector of the weak and vulnerable among his subjects. Written in an archaic script which harks back to the written pronouncements of the kings of Akkad several centuries earlier, the inscription originally contained some 275 to 300 laws, framed by a prologue and epilogue. We cannot be sure of the exact number of laws because the last seven columns of the text on the front of the monument were erased by the Elamites. We can, however, determine almost all the contents of the missing clauses from the numerous copies and duplicates of the document that have survived.

From Susa the French excavators took Hammurabi's stele to Paris where it is now on display in the Louvre. It was but one of many such pillars inscribed with Hammurabi's Laws set up on the king's orders throughout his realm, probably in all its most important temples. None of the others have survived, certainly not *in situ*, though fragments of what appear to be two of them were found in Susa during the French excavations. But copies of the actual text of the Laws, or extracts from it, do survive, in varying states of preservation, unearthed from numerous sites throughout Mesopotamia. Some date to Hammurabi's time, or to the reigns of his dynastic successors. But others belong to much later periods—indeed some as late as the Neo-Assyrian and Neo-Babylonian periods in the 7th and 6th centuries BC.

This is not to say that the laws themselves remained in force, or indeed had any legal status, through all these centuries (whatever force or status they may originally have had—a matter to which we shall return). Rather, they achieved the status of a literary classic in the scribal repertoire of the kingdoms and civilizations that succeeded the Old Babylonian world. They became an integral part of a scribal education for centuries to come. This ensured that they were copied repeatedly by successive generations of scribes—and that copies, or fragments of copies, from many different eras have survived to the present day.

The nature and content of the Laws

The Laws framed by the prologue and epilogue were compiled and publicly made known in the very last years of Hammurabi's long reign, probably his thirty-ninth year (i.e. the late 1750s). In both prologue and epilogue, especially the latter, the king emphasizes his role as the dispenser of justice throughout his land, and as the protector of the weakest members of society, those most vulnerable to exploitation and wrongdoing, like the waif and the widow. His divine appointment also required him to be a great builder, and the prologue tells us how he fulfilled this obligation, by restoring and enriching his land's cities, especially their shrines, temples, and sanctuaries. But above all, the image Hammurabi presents to us is that of a king who rules his people justly, wisely, and compassionately.

Hammurabi had highlighted this as a prime responsibility of kingship very early in his reign by labelling his second year upon the throne as the one in which he 'established justice in the land'. 'Justice' is here a translation of the Babylonian term *mīšarum*, a royal edict issued periodically by a king for the purpose of relieving social and economic hardship among his subjects. He did so by announcing a general remission of debts when the burden of indebtedness became widespread and threatened the economic stability of a whole society. The *mīšarum* provided a specific instance of the king's proclaimed responsibility of extending his protection to those most in need of it at times of particular stress. Hammurabi issued a *mīšarum* again in the twenty-second year of rule. And his dynastic successors, beginning with Samsu-iluna, continued to make periodic pronouncements of this kind.

The overall concepts and ideology underpinning the Laws were not in themselves highly innovatory. They were largely inspired by, and sometimes modelled on, legal texts compiled by three earlier kings—Ur-Namma of the Ur III dynasty, Lipit-Ishtar of the Isin dynasty, and Dadusha, king of Eshnunna. Like Hammurabi's, the legal texts of these kings showed great concern for protecting the weak and the vulnerable. In this respect, then, Hammurabi was carrying on an already established tradition of legal reform, even adopting a similar form of wording in his Laws. Like their predecessors, Hammurabi's Laws are expressed as conditional statements: *If* (someone does/suffers something), *then* (this will be the consequence). In content as well as in their form of expression, many of Hammurabi's laws maintain long-established legal traditions.

But some differ significantly from their predecessors in the stipulations they make. The most striking examples are those that embody the *lex talionis* principle—revenge for revenge's sake, or in biblical terms, 'an eye for an eye, a tooth for a tooth'. Thus, if a builder constructs a house for a man which is so unstable that it collapses and kills the householder, the builder shall be put to death (Laws of Hammurabi (LH) 229). If the victim happens to be the householder's son, then a son of the builder shall be put to death (LH 230). Such clauses may hark back to an earlier nomadic stage of Amorite society when punishments of the *lex talionis* type were perhaps a regular means of dispensing justice. We do not know how literally or frequently the *lex talionis* principle was applied in the urban communities of Old Babylonian society. It did, however, provide a precedent for similar provisions in Old Testament law.

In seeking to ensure justice for the land, the Hammurabic Laws cover a number of criminal activities, including assault, theft, robbery, criminal negligence, and homicide. But other provisions cover civil and commercial activities within society, such as sales and rentals of real estate, inheritance rights, and hire rates for equipment and labourers. Also, a number of clauses have to do with marriage provisions, divorce, and inheritance rights, particularly because of the all-important question of property settlements and transfers which marriages and their outcomes entailed. In their coverage of these and many other matters, the Laws contain a wide range of information about Babylonian society in this period, including the kingdom's social structure, its agricultural and economic activities, the professions and crafts that underpinned its material and cultural development, the merchandise that formed the basis of its commercial activity, and the acquisition of slaves and the role they played in society.

The social hierarchy

One of the most important aspects of the Laws is the information they provide about the hierarchy within Babylonian society. First, there was a class of people designated by the term *awīlum*. Commonly translated as 'free person', this term covered a wide range of individuals of varying social status, from the more elite professional classes, presumably including scribes, to craftsmen and artisans. Though it is clear that there was a social hierarchy within the *awīlum* category, the term was in its broadest sense applied to many people of free, independent status. Such people were often closely associated with the palace. Sometimes they were appointed to senior positions in the palace bureaucracy. But if so, they owed their appointments to the king, and presumably to their own ability. They did not hold them as a hereditary right. The term *awīlum* certainly does not in itself designate membership of an aristocratic class in Babylonian society, though in some cases it appears to be used of an elite, privileged group within this society—hence the term 'gentleman' which is sometimes used to translate it.

From the palace, the *awīlum* and his family received grants of land, called *prebends* by modern scholars (which could include farmland and orchards and houses on the estate), from whose produce they often derived their main means of support. But the grants also came with obligations imposed upon their beneficiaries to provide certain goods or services to the palace. These could range from paying it a proportion of an estate's produce, supplying labour for estates still directly worked by the palace, or performing other duties for the king, such as military service. In a number of cases, the prebends stayed within the same family, passing from father to son—so in this sense at least there was an hereditary dimension to an *awīlum*'s position. The service the *awīlum* was obliged to perform was known as *ilkum*-service. This term was linked with the allotments of land which the king granted his subjects at all levels of society for the services which the recipients rendered to him, sometimes of a civil, sometimes of a military nature. Those who fought in the king's armies were usually paid with an *ilkum*-field, from which they derived their living when not on campaign. And they were obliged to ensure that the land they received was exploited to its maximum agricultural extent as a contribution to the kingdom's overall food production.

An *awīlum* often contracted out the land granted to him under this system to other people of free but lower status. These formed the largest component of the population of Babylonian towns and cities. They were designated by the term *muškēnum*, often translated as 'commoner'. But as Eva von Dassow points out, both an *awīlum* and a *muškēnum* could be wealthy or poor, and both could receive benefits from or provide services to the state; the main distinction was that the *muškēnū* (plural form) were subordinate to authority, while the *awīlū* (plural) exercised it, constituting the assembly and serving as magistrates.

The *muškēnum* depended largely on his own personal resources to make a living, by hiring himself out as an agricultural labourer, or by working as a tenant the land contracted out to him either by an *awīlum*, or directly by the palace. In good times, the land provided sufficient produce to support him and his family, with a large enough surplus to pay the landlord or lessor, and thus fulfil the obligations of his tenancy. Alternatively, like the *awīlum*, he received a land-grant from the king which he worked to provide himself and his family with a living, in exchange for services to the king, including perhaps his own labour on the palace estates. In hard times, such as a long period of drought, he might struggle for survival, either through being deprived of his income, or falling into debt because he was unable to pay the rent on a plot of land he had leased. If his tenancy was extended to give him the chance to make good the deficit, a succession of bad years would have simply increased his debt-obligations.

Alternatively, a *muškēnum* who had land of his own might be forced to take out a loan against it when it failed to produce enough to support him. Interest rates were apparently very high—for example, 20 per cent on silver loans and 33.3 per cent on barley loans. If he was unable to repay the loan, he would have to hand over his land to his creditor and rent it back from him. If he then failed to pay the rent, he was plunged into even greater debt. It was in response to such situations that a king sometimes issued a *mīšarum* decree, which proclaimed a general remission of debts for his subjects, as a short-term measure to relieve economic distress when it had become widespread throughout his land—for example, during periods of prolonged drought and poor harvests.

At times when there was no remission of debts, a debtor who had no chance of fulfilling his financial obligations to his creditor could be forced to sell himself and/or other members of his family into slavery to his creditor. This was apparently a common predicament, affecting particularly the *muškēnum* class, who lacked the kinds of protection enjoyed by the *awīlum* class because of the latter's palace connections. One of the provisions of Hammurabi's Laws did limit to three years the term of debt-slavery which obliged a debtor or other members of his family to serve in the household of his creditor (LH 117). But while this may have eased the disastrous economic effects that unlimited debt-slavery could have had on society, it did not in itself help alleviate the conditions that had led to debt-slavery in the first place. In bad times, a *muškēnum* could be a highly vulnerable member of the community to which he belonged.

The slave

The third and lowest category of persons referred to in Hammurabi's Laws were the *wardum* and *amtum*, terms used for a male and female slave respectively. (*Wardum* was also used more generally to designate a person in a subordinate relationship to someone of higher status. Thus a high court official could be designated as a *wardum* or 'slave' or 'servant' of the king.) Apart from those temporarily enslaved by their fellow countrymen for failing to pay their debts, slaves were acquired through trading operations by Babylonian merchants abroad or through the importation of prisoners-of-war acquired as booty on military campaigns. Most of the latter seem to have become property of the king, who housed them in special barracks and used them on public construction projects or assigned them as temple employees. A number of private slaves, apparently marked out by some sort of distinctive 'slave-hairlock' (LH 146), were employed within the household on domestic duties and basic tasks such as grinding flour. Female slaves were assigned the job of weaving clothes for the members of their household.

As we saw, people who worked in a household as debt-slaves, and were probably Babylonians themselves, were released after several years of servitude. Other slaves acquired from outside Babylonia through trade or as war booty could remain slaves for the rest of their lives, and their offspring born in their owner's household were slaves from birth. That such persons, as well as state-owned slaves, sometimes sought to escape is indicated by the Laws, which prescribe harsh penalties for those who harboured escapees, and rewards for those who captured and restored them to their owners (LH 16, 17). Yet the life of a privately owned slave seems not often to have been a burdensome one, and there was always the possibility of manumission.

Marriages within and between classes

At this point, let's turn our attention to a pronouncement in the Laws that makes reference to all three of the classes we have previously discussed. It states that if a palace-slave or a commoner's slave marries a woman of the *awīlum*-class who then has children, the slave's owner cannot claim ownership of these children (LH 175).

This is one of a fairly substantial group of provisions in the Laws which have to do with marriage. They are concerned above all with practicalities such as bride-price, inheritance rights, and the disposal of possessions that came with a marriage (such as the bride's dowry) or were accrued in a marriage, in the event of a divorce or the death of one of the marriage-partners. A particularly noteworthy aspect of these laws is the provisions they make for marriage between persons of different status, slave and free. That the Laws deal with such situations indicates that there were no legal impediments to such marriages, and that they did in fact occur. What we don't know is how frequently they occurred. Nor do we have clear answers to the questions they obviously raise. For example, what reasons could there have been for a woman of the *awīlum*-class to marry a slave, or for the slave's owner to consent to such a marriage? For the latter in particular the incentives must have been fairly considerable—since as the clause stipulates, the offspring of the union would be free, whereas offspring resulting from the union of two of an owner's slaves would automatically become and remain the property of their parents' owner.

Further provisions in the Laws (LH 176a and b) cover the situation where an *awīlum*-woman actually enters into her slave-husband's household, whether the slave be the property of the palace or of a commoner. The wife may even bring a dowry with her. What happens to the dowry and any possessions accumulated by the marriage-partners during their marriage if the slave-husband dies? The Laws state that if a dowry has been brought by the woman, it should revert to her, and that any property accumulated by the pair during their marriage should be equally divided between the deceased slave's owner and the slave's widow, on behalf of the children of the marriage. It is clear, then, that the slave's marriage to a free person did nothing to change his slave status, though his children would be free from birth, and inheritance-wise be treated fairly in the distribution of property after their father's death.

More generally, Hammurabi's marriage provisions have much to do with 'gifts', or property which forms part of the marriage arrangement. At the very least, some form of legal contract had to be entered into for a marriage to be considered valid (LH 128). A number of clauses refer to the payment by a bridegroom-to-be of a 'bridewealth' to his prospective father-in-law prior to the marriage. This served as a kind of guarantee, both by the bridegroom and his father-in-law on accepting it, that both parties would abide by the arrangement they had made. It seems to have been part of a traditional pre-nuptial ceremony, though we cannot tell from the Laws whether the presentation of a 'bridewealth' gift was a *regular* prelude to marriage. Also, it was the custom for a bride to bring with her a dowry which, in the normal course of events, remained in her new household without ever actually coming under her husband's control or into his possession. This we learn from clauses which deal with property issues that arise in the event of a marriage ending.

By and large, marriages were monogamous, and fidelity in marriage was expected, especially from the woman. If, for example, she was caught *in flagrante delicto* with a man not her husband, both the lovers were to submit to what is called the 'River Ordeal'. We do not know what the nature of this 'ordeal' was. But from LH 129, it appears that if it demonstrated the guilt of both parties (apparently it did not kill them in the process), the cuckolded husband could not ask the king to impose the death penalty on his wife's lover unless he agreed to the same penalty for his wife. The Hittite compendium of laws contains a similar provision. On the other hand, if a husband accused his wife of adultery without evidence to support his claim, a simple denial by his wife was sufficient to absolve her of any guilt and ensure that she remained in her husband's household (LH 131). Not so, apparently, if she was accused by someone else. In this case, she must submit to the River Ordeal to prove her innocence (LH 132). These last two clauses in particular seem to reflect specific past cases, and the unknown circumstances which led to the judgments in these cases must have been rather more complex than is indicated by the bald text of the Laws.

Another ground for a husband to divorce his wife was if she failed to provide him with children. Should he seek divorce on these grounds, and the wife was in other respects blameless (indeed in this respect too she may not have been the one at fault, though the Laws do not admit this possibility), he must provide her with adequate compensation before dismissing her from his house (to make way for a second and hopefully fertile wife). Compensation took the form of an amount of silver equivalent to the bridewealth he originally paid when he contracted the marriage, and the return of her dowry (LH 138). This is in contrast to the treatment of a wife who is extravagant, speaks ill of her husband, and abandons him. Such behaviour provides grounds for the husband to divorce her and dismiss her from his household without any compensation whatsoever. Alternatively, he may decide not to divorce her, and may then take another wife in her place, relegating wife no. 1 to the position of a slave in his house (LH 141). But the law is not entirely one-sided. A woman may seek divorce from her husband if he is wayward and verbally abuses her. If she takes the matter to court and receives a judgment in her favour, the divorce will be granted, and she may return to her father's household, taking her dowry with her (LH 142).

In keeping with one of the Laws' principal concerns—to protect society's most vulnerable members—several of the laws make provision for wives whose husbands have been captured, presumably by the enemy during military campaigns. There may well have been a welfare system in operation to support the widows of those killed in combat as well as those missing in action. This is not attested in the Laws, but the Laws do acknowledge the plight of a wife whose husband has failed to return home because he has been taken prisoner. In this case, the wife may without committing an offence take up residence in the household of another man, presumably with her children, if she would otherwise be left destitute (LH 134). There is a follow-up clause (LH 135) which states that if the husband regains his freedom and returns from captivity, his wife must go back to him; but any children resulting from her period of cohabitation with the other man will inherit the property of their natural father.

Protecting the rights of heirs is a significant concern of the Laws. It can apply to an *awīlum*'s children by a slave woman as well as by his 'first-ranking wife'. If the man acknowledges as his own any children he has by the slave woman, they shall share equally in their father's estate with the children of the first-ranking wife, though a son of the latter will be the 'preferred heir' and take first pick of the estate (LH 170). Even if the father does not formally acknowledge his children by a slave woman, they along with their mother are to be freed on their father's death, and not continue as slave members of his first-ranking wife's household (LH 171).

Justice was not blind

Though the Laws were concerned with ensuring justice to all members of society, Hammurabic justice was not even-handed in its treatment of those of the different classes who came within its purview. This is particularly evident in the clauses that deal with criminal offences. The penalties imposed upon an offender varied according to both the class to which he belonged and that to which the victim belonged. Thus if an *awīlum* blinds another *awīlum* or breaks his bone, the offender shall suffer the same fate—on the *lex talionis* principle (LH 196–7). If, however, the *awīlum* inflicts the same injury on a *muškēnum*, he will suffer only a monetary penalty—sixty shekels of silver (LH 198). And if he inflicts the same injury on an *awīlum*'s slave, he shall hand over half the slave's value in silver (to the owner, presumably) (LH 199). A lesser form of assault ('striking the cheek' is specified) by one member of the *awīlum* class against another of the same status attracts a penalty of sixty shekels of silver (LH 203). But if the victim is of a higher status of *awīlum*, then his offender's punishment will be a public flogging (LH 202). And an *awīlum*'s slave who 'strikes the cheek' of a member of the *awīlum* class suffers the loss of his ear (LH 205).

What access to justice did a Babylonian really have?

An important reason for Hammurabi's command that numerous monuments bearing his Laws be set up in the cities of his kingdom was to ensure that as many of his subjects as possible had access to the Laws' provisions and could seek justice on this basis. Thus the king states in the Epilogue of the Laws that any man who believes he has been wronged in a lawsuit should come before the king's stele and statue, and have read out to him the provisions which the stele contains. These will make clear to him whether or not he has been treated justly.

For any of Hammurabi's subjects who had limited reading and writing skills, or none at all, this was to be no bar to their learning of their rights from the king's pronouncements. Provision is made for scribes to read out to those who were largely or entirely illiterate—or for that matter to anyone at all—any of the Laws' statements relevant to a legal situation in which they were involved and on which they sought advice. Possibly, consultants had to hire their own readers for this purpose. But the readers may have been palace-appointees who were stationed next to the monument, perhaps on a roster basis, to ensure there was always one or more on hand to deal with what may well have been a constant queue of enquirers seeking information on the Laws' contents.

Yet what did all this mean in practical terms? Could enquirers always find a clause or clauses that dealt specifically with a matter on which they sought advice? And in any case, what could they *actually do* with the information provided to them by the Laws? First, scholars no longer use the term 'Code' in referring to the Laws, for this term implies a systematic and comprehensive collection of statutes that cover all possible legal situations, whether of a criminal or a civil nature. In fact, the Laws are far from comprehensive in the situations they cover (they provide a mere sampling of cases that might involve legal action) and are sometimes contradictory. Nor do they make any clear distinction between civil and criminal law. On top of all this, they seem not to have been binding in any way on the courts of the land.

Here let us stress a very important point. The Laws on their own provide only a partial picture of Old Babylonian society. Contemporary legal and administrative documents and letters are at least as important in formulating a more complete overview of this society. These documents often provide us with specific instances of the Babylonian system of justice in practice. Hundreds of letters relating to legal matters were written by individual citizens to various authorities responsible for the administration of justice, including the king himself. And hundreds of letters also survive which the king wrote to his regional governors, many providing instructions on a range of legal cases referred to him for advice. Decisions made by courts on matters brought before them for judgment were recorded and passed on to successful litigants for future reference if the matters again became the subject of legal action. While the Laws provide the focus of this chapter, letters and other legal and administrative documents greatly supplement the information they contain—about the class-structure of

Babylonian society, the central importance of the family in Babylonian life, provisions relating to commercial transactions, property and inheritance rights, and the role and treatment of slaves.

The king was Chief Justice of the land, though the great majority of cases brought to his court were tried by his representatives. On occasions, the king himself presided over appeals against decisions made by a lower court. Many documents set out a sequence of the procedures followed in judging a case and reaching a decision on the matter. These provide us with first-hand information on the day-to-day administration of justice in the kingdom. Sometimes the local authorities sought advice from the king on a particular case, and his response was contained in one of the many letters he wrote to them.

By way of illustration, a letter from Hammurabi's successor Samsu-iluna deals with two cases referred to the king by the authorities at Sippar. Both concern the *nadiātum*, religious women attending to the duties of the temple of Shamash. In one of them, the authorities in charge of the women had complained that the people of Sippar had let their daughters enter the cloister without providing any means of subsistence for them; they were thus feeding themselves from the stores in the temple. In his response, the king set out the obligations the relatives of these women would henceforth be required to fulfil, as a condition of the women being allowed to enter the cloister, or remain living in it. But the response is framed in general terms (beginning, like the Laws, with an 'If' clause), so that the judicial authorities were provided with a ruling not just for this case, but for all cases of a similar nature that might arise in the future.

The purpose of the Laws

This brings us back to the question of what purpose, in practical terms, the Laws actually served in Babylonian society. Before addressing this question, we should ask a related one: Why were the Laws gathered together in a single corpus in the first place? An answer that readily springs to mind is that they were essentially a collection of legal precedents—a case was judged, a decision handed down, and the case and verdict were recorded for possible reference in future trials. Most importantly, the fundamental purpose of the Laws was to highlight Hammurabi's role as a divinely appointed ruler whose prime concern was to ensure that justice prevailed throughout his land, and that all his subjects alike were entitled to protection under its laws.

In practice, Hammurabi's Laws functioned not as a manual of prescriptive rulings, but rather as a source of guidance and a set of guidelines—embodying important principles of justice—for the good governance of society. To be sure, a number of the penalties to which they refer are extremely harsh, with death and mutilation stipulated for a wide range of offences. Possibly, many such penalties reflect an earlier period of Amorite tribal tradition, when society was more vulnerable to those who violated its norms. But they dispelled the notion that might is right, with emphasis instead on ensuring that protection was provided for all members of society, including the weakest and most vulnerable among them. The fact that this was so strongly emphasized not only by Hammurabi, but also by his predecessors in social reform, makes clear that such a notion in early societies was not one that could simply be taken for granted.

Chapter 3
Old Babylonian cities

Imagine that you have been transported back in time almost 4,000 years and set down in Hammurabi's capital. What would Babylon have looked like then? Growing up as a small settlement on the Euphrates river or a branch of it, Babylon was at least seven centuries old when Hammurabi came to power. Its origins date back to the middle of the third millennium BC. But it was not until the reign of Hammurabi that Babylon had its first flowering as one of the great royal capitals of the Near Eastern world.

Unfortunately, we have very few material remains of the royal city from this period (though it was almost certainly a good deal smaller than it was in later times). This is because much of it was removed and built over in later periods. The little that does remain of the city is largely inaccessible to archaeologists because of the rise of the underground water table. The first major excavations on the site, conducted by the Deutsche Orient-Gesellschaft (German Oriental Society) between 1899 and 1917 under Robert Koldewey's direction, concentrated on the site's upper levels, most notably the Neo-Babylonian one when Babylon was the capital of Nebuchadnezzar II's kingdom.

But between 1907 and 1932, excavations of the Old Babylonian city were carried out in the area called the Merkes which lay in what is now referred to as the 'eastern new city' adjoining the city's innermost areas. The remains of a few houses were identified here, and from them a small number of tablets were retrieved. Otherwise, archaeological investigations have revealed very little about the Hammurabic city. The palace itself, the administrative centre of the whole kingdom, seems to have completely disappeared. From documentary evidence, we learn that at this time the city was defended by walls, like most Babylonian cities of the period, and contained many temples, attested in the year-name formulae of the kings of Hammurabi's dynasty. They included the Esangila, Babylon's most important religious precinct, and temples dedicated to a number of deities among whom the most important were Enlil, Marduk, Shamash, Ishtar, and Adad.

But we have no material remains of these temples, at least none that are as yet accessible. Indeed evidence from Babylon itself is extremely sparse, and though overall the Old Babylonian period is a well-attested one, our most substantial knowledge of Babylon and Babylonia comes from other sites in the kingdom—and from cities and kingdoms outside Babylonia. This includes written records, most famously Hammurabi's stele itself, rediscovered in the Elamite city Susa. We learn more about what Old Babylonian cities looked like from other urban sites in the kingdom, notably Ur and Uruk in its southern part.

Capital of the late third-millennium Ur III empire, the city of Ur remained an important religious and commercial centre throughout the Old Babylonian period. In this period, much restoration work was carried out in the city's religious precincts, and new residential areas were developed. Here and in the city of Nippur in particular, excavations have given us a fairly clear picture of what a major city in Babylonia looked like during the Old Babylonian period. Despite earlier conclusions that these cities were laid out on a regular grid pattern with straight intersecting avenues, archaeological evidence indicates that their main thoroughfares were narrow, winding streets. These connected with smaller streets and alleyways, crowded and noisy, which the local inhabitants had to pass through to enter the blocks of residential buildings where they and their families lived.

The houses were made of unbaked, sundried mudbrick, though some of the more upmarket residences had a baked brick lower course to protect them against erosion. They were generally built closely together, often with adjoining party walls, and entered from the street or alleyway through a narrow door. However, residences of wealthy citizens built in the Merkes area of Babylon, and no doubt in similar public spaces in other Babylonian cities, were accessed from larger streets or perhaps even from public squares. Otherwise, the houses were shut off from the outside world by blank, windowless walls—for security against the throngs of passers-by as well as to keep out the heat and the dust. To compensate, their interiors contained at least one courtyard (two or three in some larger residences), around which the rooms of the dwelling were built. These rooms were sheltered from the elements by flat roofs which consisted of a layer of woven reeds and on top of it an outer covering of clay mixed with straw.

Clearly, the materials of which most houses were entirely composed would have rendered them highly vulnerable to weather conditions and other environmental factors, necessitating a complete makeover—replastering the house—each year. Timber was obviously an expensive commodity (since trees were rare phenomena in Babylonia), and was only occasionally used, sometimes as panels in doors. The courtyards, open to the sky, provided light and ventilation for the houses, and probably served as both recreational and work areas. Thus Harriet Crawford comments, who also notes the wide variation in the size of the individual houses unearthed in Ur, ranging from 9.68 to 19.25 square metres (similarly at Nippur). Differences in size between the various houses no doubt reflect the material circumstances and status of the individual householders. But large houses were not merely show-places, designed to display their owners' wealth and status. They served also as headquarters for the various work enterprises in which their owners engaged.

Sometimes, houses of different size adjoined or were in close proximity to one another in the residential areas. This has led to the suggestion that it was not social class or degree of affluence that defined the residential areas. Rather, the clusters of residences of different sizes in the various areas reflect occupation by related family groups, many of whom may have followed the same profession or trade as a family tradition.

The Babylonian diet could be a rich and varied one, if you had the means to sample all that was on offer. There was an abundance of fish, and sometimes shrimps and crayfish available from the fishmongers, and from other vendors a large variety of fruit (like dates, figs, apples, and pomegranates), duck eggs, and vegetables (like lettuce, cucumbers, onions, chickpeas, and turnips). Meat products, like lamb, beef, and goat, were also available—though meat was a much less common, and more expensive item in the Babylonian diet. When in season, locusts made into a fermented sauce added further taste and variety to this diet. And all could be washed down with one of the local beers, or on special occasions with wine imported from northern Mesopotamia (at a hefty price!). Herbs and spices were used to flavour these beverages.

Much of the day-to-day business of merchants, traders, craftsmen, and others engaged in earning a living was conducted near the city's gates, often in market stalls just inside or outside the gates. These were also the centre of much social interaction, particularly, we might imagine, between the city's residents and travellers coming from other parts of Babylonia or further afield. The travellers had been engaged in trading enterprises and other activities, perhaps as representatives of family businesses based in the city to which they were now returning. The news they had gathered in the course of their travels would have assured them of a warm welcome on their return.

The city gates were an important part of the city's defences, for most cities were protected by imposing fortifications. A significant proportion of the population attached to a city either lived in peripheral settlements beyond its walls or else worked on plots of land or estates outside them, as tenant farmers, as land-grantees, or as employees of land-owners; the land-owners included the palace, or the local administration which governed the city on the king's behalf. Cultivated land, including orchards and date palm plantations, could extend right up to the walls, and indeed such cultivated areas would sometimes be found within the walls. For those who lived in the peripheral 'suburbs' outside the gates, an alarm-system would presumably have warned them of the approach of an enemy, hopefully in time for these 'suburbanites' to move themselves and their livestock inside the walls, or to some other nearby fortified area which offered at least a temporary haven.

Socially, commercially, and strategically, the gates were the most distinctive feature of their city's fortifications. But they were also potentially the most vulnerable parts of it to enemy attack. For even if a besieging army failed to penetrate the walls via the gates or by any other means, it could block the gates, thus preventing persons or merchandise entering or leaving the city. A successful gate-blockade could eventually force the city to capitulate if it were deprived of access to supplies essential to life. Gates could be located both on the landward side of a city and on the city's main river-routes or harbours.

All Babylonia's important urban centres were located either on one of the two main rivers, the Tigris and the Euphrates, or on canals and waterways which were linked to them. The harbours or quays were often areas of intense commercial activity for transporting goods to and from the city, both north and south of Babylonia. Already in the period of the Akkadian empire, the Mesopotamian waterways gave access to regular trading links with the countries to the south, along the Persian Gulf (for example, Magan at its southern end) and the Arabian Sea and the lands beyond (for example, Meluhha). Items imported from these lands included wood, copper, and semi-precious stones from Magan, and gold, silver, carnelian, lapis lazuli, and a black wood (perhaps ebony) from Meluhha. (The imports from Meluhha probably originated in other lands.)

We have noted that one of the king's chief responsibilities was the restoration of the temples of the gods throughout his realm as well as the construction of new temples. Each city had a major temple, or temple precinct dedicated to its patron or tutelary deity—Marduk in Babylon, Enlil in Nippur, Inanna (Ishtar) in Uruk, Nanna (Sīn) in Ur. The city often contained temples dedicated to other deities as well. As one of the two dominant institutions of Babylonian society, the temple enjoyed a role equal to that of the palace in the influence it exercised on the social, cultural, and political life of Babylonian society. And as a major owner of food-producing land in Babylonia's largely agriculture-based economy, the temple institution played a substantial part in the kingdom's overall economy. The city's main temple (at least) could occupy a precinct which spread over several acres and incorporated several buildings, including the shrine which housed the deity, the courtyard where ceremonies honouring the deity were performed, and numerous rooms which stored the cultic paraphernalia associated with the worship of the gods and the festivals held in their honour.

The most striking monument you would see on your visit to Babylon, and indeed a feature of a number of Babylonian cities, was a structure known as a ziggurat (Figure 4). This took the form of a stepped building, consisting of between three and seven levels, each one smaller in area than the one below it, and ascending pyramid-like towards the heavens. We do not know what precisely the purpose or significance of a ziggurat was, beyond the fact that it was clearly a special type of sacred building. One suggestion is that it served as a substitute for the mountains

4. Reconstruction of the ziggurat at Ur (third millennium BC).

in which the gods originally lived. The earliest ziggurats date to the third millennium BC, and all the chief cities of Babylonia had at least one. Sometimes they stood within a temple precinct of the main god, sometimes they were in a precinct of their own. The ziggurat of Babylon lay in the cultic precinct known as Etemenanki. It became notorious in biblical tradition as the 'tower of Babel'. In this tradition, God was so angered by the construction of such a monument to human arrogance that he scattered the peoples responsible for it over the whole earth and 'confused their language' so that they could never again understand or collaborate with one another (Gen. 11: 1–9).

Chapter 4

The Kassites:
(c.1570–1155 BC)

The arrival of the Kassites

The Hittite sack of Babylon around 1595 brought the Old Babylonian Kingdom to an end, and left for a time a political power vacuum in the region over which the Hammurabic dynasty had held sway. Already under its last rulers, threats to the kingdom's existence were emerging, particularly from the Hurrians in northern Mesopotamia and northern Syria. But the first people who actually asserted their dominance over the territories of the former kingdom, some time after the destruction of Babylon, were a group from the marshlands of the south. They were called the Sealanders. Already by the reign of Hammurabi's successor Samsu-iluna the Sealanders seem to have been a disruptive force in Babylonia. Subsequently in the kingdom's later years they may have established some degree of control over the southern part of Babylonia, and perhaps all the way north to Nippur. There's a further possibility that a king of the Sealand called Gulkishar captured Babylon itself, or what was left of it, and occupied its throne. But the evidence for this, which appears in a fragmentary Babylonian text after the end of the Old Babylonian kingdom, is questionable.

In any case, for perhaps as much as a century the Sealanders prevented the domination of Babylonia by another group who subsequently held sway over the whole of Babylonia until the very end of the Late Bronze Age. From a homeland perhaps on the Eurasian steppe lands or in the Zagros mountain region, this group had spread widely through Babylonia and neighbouring regions by the end of the Old Babylonian Kingdom, settling among the existing inhabitants in a generally peaceful manner (Figure 5). They called themselves the *Galzu*, but we refer to them as Kassites—from *kaššū*, the Akkadianized form of their name. They were but one of a number of immigrant groups who had settled in Babylonia by this time; there were also groups of Assyrians, Elamites, forerunners of the Aramaeans, and other peoples. But the Kassites were clearly distinguished from all of them by their language.

Unfortunately, very little is known about this language, for it survives mainly in proper names, including those of many Kassite kings, the remains of a couple of Akkadian–Kassite lexicons, a few scraps of other texts, and an occasional Kassite word in other sources. Meagre though this information is, it is sufficient to tell us that the Kassite language was totally unrelated to Akkadian, or any other Semitic language. One of the names which may be Kassite in origin is that by which Babylonia was widely known under Kassite rule. The kings of the contemporary Near Eastern kingdoms referred to their Kassite counterparts in Babylonia as 'the kings of the land of Karduniash'.

An important reason why little of the Kassite language has survived is that Kassite kings, and no doubt the Kassite population as a whole, rapidly assimilated to the prevailing language and customs of their adopted homeland. They used Babylonian (and also Sumerian) for their texts and inscriptions. And they not only maintained but strengthened and reinvigorated the traditions of this new homeland. Their ethnic distinctiveness also became increasingly blurred by their intermarriages with the local peoples, and by diplomatic marriage-alliances between members of their royal dynasty and the families of their

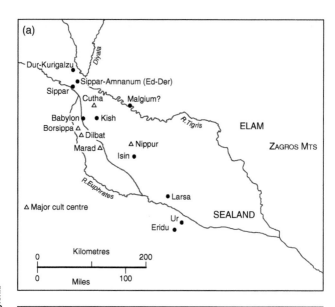

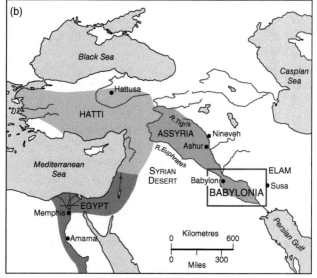

5. (a) Babylonia under Kassite rule; (b) Kassite Babylonia and the contemporary 'Great Kingdoms'.

international peers. Further obscuring the ethnic origins of the Kassite royal line was the assumption of Babylonian names by five of its last seven kings.

Unfortunately, the Kassite period in Babylonian history, though a lengthy and extremely significant one, is not well covered by written sources. Only about 1,500 texts have so far been published to document it. And almost none of them date to the first two centuries or so of the Kassite period; this means that we have to rely on a few scraps of information, and a good deal of speculation, about how the Kassites eventually won control of Babylon, and subsequently extended their sway through all Babylonia. Based on what we do know, much of the credit for this seems to have been due to an early fifteenth-century Kassite king called Ulamburiash, whose achievements included the imposition of his authority over southern Babylonia, long ruled by the so-called Sealand Dynasty. Under Ulamburiash and his successors, the whole of Babylonia, as well as peripheral regions to the east and south of it, was united into a single state.

Nationhood under the Kassites

Scholars are pretty well agreed on what they see as the greatest benefit bestowed on Babylonia by the Kassite dynasty: the gift of nationhood. Earlier, Hammurabi had extended his rule throughout Babylonia, which became politically subject to him and (to a diminishing extent) his successors. Even so, the city-states of the region saw themselves as independent of one another, with no overriding sense of national unity binding them together. Until the Kassite period, Babylonia as a nation did not in fact exist. From then on, the kingdom of Babylonia was a clearly defined territory with distinct borders. And some scholars would argue that it is only now that we can appropriately use the term 'Babylonia' to define southern Mesopotamia. The unification of Babylonia, and the strong stability of the region under Kassite rule, ensured that kings of the dynasty who held sway over it were ranked as members of the elite club of Great Kings of the Near Eastern world. Their peers were the rulers of Hatti (Kingdom of the Hittites), Egypt, and Mittani (later replaced by Assyria). (The heartland of both Mittani and Assyria occupied much of northern Mesopotamia.) All spoke of each other as 'Great Kings' and addressed each other as 'My Brother'. Significantly, it was in the Kassite period that Babylonian became the international language of diplomacy throughout the Late Bronze Age Near Eastern world.

It was no doubt the Babylonian state's strong political unity and stability that underpinned the great flowering of its cultural and scientific institutions. These were not innovations, but rather the further evolution and development of earlier institutions evident in the period of the Old Babylonian Kingdom at its peak. Kassite kings applied themselves enthusiastically to the task of preserving, nurturing, and further developing the customs and institutions of their adopted land, while in the process practically all traces of their own culture disappeared. Undoubtedly, the political stability which the Kassites brought to their rule in Babylonia and their respect for the traditions and customs of those upon whom they imposed it provided a peaceful, secure environment within the land, which helped ensure that the arts and sciences flourished, in such fields as literature, medicine, mathematics, astronomy, music, art, and architecture.

One important innovation of the Kassite regime was the establishment of a new administrative capital of the kingdom, at what is now called Aqar Quf. Located just west of modern Baghdad, on the site of earlier fortress settlements built in the Ur III and Old Babylonian periods, the new city was named Dur-Kurigalzu—Fort Kurigalzu—after its founder, the Kassite king Kurigalzu I (late fifteenth century to c.1374). Constructed on a significantly larger scale than the earlier settlements there, the new capital was just one of the major building projects undertaken by Kurigalzu. Ur, Eridu, and Uruk were among other Babylonian cities that benefited from his building programme. We cannot be sure why he built a new capital for the kingdom. There may well have been practical strategic measures of a commercial or military nature behind its establishment. Certainly, it seems in no way to have diminished the prestige of Babylon, which remained the kingdom's ceremonial and religious centre (and indeed the focus for many of its commercial and political activities), much as Ashur remained the ceremonial centre of the Assyrian kingdom when new Assyrian capitals were built at Nineveh and Nimrud.

The Kassites on the international scene

Diplomatic and commercial relations with Egypt had already been established by this time, and these were subsequently maintained or renewed by the Babylonian king Kadashman-Enlil I (*c.*1374–1360). We know this from several exchanges of correspondence between Kadashman-Enlil and the pharaoh Amenhotep III. Babylonia emerged more clearly as a player on the international scene during the reign of Kadashman-Enlil's successor Burnaburiash II (*c.*1359–1333). This was at a time when the kingdom of Mittani was locked into a struggle to the death with Hatti, whose throne was then occupied by the formidable warlord Suppiluliuma I. Suppiluliuma's progressive conquest of Mittani's territories, including its heartland in northern Mesopotamia, provided Burnaburiash with the opportunity for expanding his kingdom northwards. But though he made some inroads into northern Mesopotamian territory, and certainly facilitated the spread of Babylonian cultural influence there, the power vacuum left by the fall of Mittani in the region was rapidly filled by a resurgent Assyrian kingdom.

Assyria's new rise to prominence was due particularly to an enterprising ruler called Ashur-uballit who ruled from about 1353 until 1318. If Suppiluliuma viewed this particular outcome of his victories against Mittani with some concern, Burnaburiash must have been considerably alarmed by it, for the aggressive new power now threatened his own kingdom, which lay immediately to its south. But first of all Ashur-uballit wanted international diplomatic recognition. Overtures by him to the Egyptian royal court, via his envoys, made clear his intention of joining the elite group of Great Kings of the age. Burnaburiash vigorously protested to the pharaoh Akhenaten about Assyria's attempts to muscle in on the international scene—for, he claimed, the Assyrians were his vassals and had no authority to approach the Egyptian court on their own initiative! But the pharaoh's cordial reception of Ashur-uballit's envoys, despite his neighbour's strong objections, made Burnaburiash realize that it would be politic of him to come to terms with the Assyrian. One way of doing so was to conclude a marriage-alliance with him. Ashur-uballit was not unwilling, and one was indeed concluded. The Assyrian sent his daughter Muballitat-Sherua to Babylon as Burnaburiash's bride-to-be.

It all turned out badly. The couple's son Kara-hardash succeeded to the Babylonian throne after his father's death, but the union between the two royal houses broke apart when the new king was assassinated by a group of his own countrymen. Thoroughly displeased at having a ruler with Assyrian blood in his veins, they put a Kassite nonentity in his place. Ashur-uballit retaliated by invading Babylonian territory, capturing Babylon, and executing the new king. He then installed another of Burnaburiash's sons on the throne, a second Kurigalzu, known as Kurigalzu the Younger (c.1332–1308). No doubt he intended the new king to be a mere puppet of the Assyrian regime. But Kurigalzu apparently proved an effective ruler in his own right. The crowning achievement of his reign was a successful campaign against the Elamites who were threatening his kingdom's eastern frontier. He topped off the campaign by capturing the Elamite capital Susa.

We might note in passing that a marriage-alliance which Burnaburiash contracted with the Hittite royal court also had an unhappy outcome. The Babylonian king had dispatched one of his daughters to Hatti, to wed Suppiluliuma, after the Hittite had made way for her by discarding his previous wife, the mother of his five sons. To judge from what we are told by one of these sons, Mursili (his father's second successor to the throne), the Babylonian princess became a pernicious influence in the royal household, and in the Hittite land in general. Her career ended ignominiously when Mursili accused her of murdering his own beloved wife, stripped her of all her offices, and banished her from the court. We do not know whether his action had any impact on Hatti's relations with Babylon.

After Kurigalzu II's installation on the Babylonian throne, tensions between Assyria and Babylonia may have eased for a time, only to flare up once more during the reign of Kurigalzu's son Nazi-Maruttash (*c*.1307–1282). Some years later, an amicable agreement appears to have been reached between Nazi-Maruttash and his Assyrian counterpart Adad-nirari I (*c*.1307–1275) over the boundaries between the kingdoms. There was peace for a time, but this provided only a brief respite in the hostilities and tensions between the kingdoms.

In terms of its military operations, Kassite Babylonia played a very limited role in the international arena outside Mesopotamia, with only occasional campaigns to the east (against Elam) and none of significance west of the Euphrates, where it clearly had no territorial ambitions. Even so, other great powers of the age, notably the Great Kings of Egypt and Hatti, accorded its kings peer status with their own rulers. It was clearly worth their while to cultivate diplomatic relations with the Babylonian court—no doubt largely because of the material and cultural benefits that close links with Babylonia could bring. At certain times too, Egyptian and Hittite kings may have considered their Babylonian 'royal brother' a useful potential, if not actual, military ally against Assyria. But this had no apparent effect in holding in check Assyria's expansionist ambitions—as was made abundantly clear by the Assyrian king Tukulti-Ninurta I (c.1244–1208). After inflicting a massive defeat on a Hittite army in northern Mesopotamia, Tukulti-Ninurta turned his attention southwards, invading Babylonian territory, subjugating the kingdom, and hauling off its king Kashtiliash IV (c.1232–1225) to Assyria in chains.

It was a short-lived triumph. Mounting opposition to Tukulti-Ninurta within his own kingdom and military defeats in other regions subject to him culminated in the king's assassination around 1208. Assyria's political instability enabled one of Kashtiliash's successors to re-establish his kingdom's independence, and the Kassite dynasty henceforth maintained its sovereignty until the mid 12th century. It was brought abruptly to an end by an Elamite invasion which terminated the reign of its last king, Enlil-nadin-ahi (c.1157–1155). With his death, the Babylonian kingdom became subject to a succession of largely insignificant dynasties until once more Assyria triumphed over it.

Kassite contributions to Near Eastern civilization and culture

Kassite Babylonia has left us with relatively little in the way of archaeological remains. As in the period of the Old Babylonian Kingdom, Babylon itself has yielded only meagre material evidence for this period since most of the Kassite level of the city, like the Old Babylonian one, is beneath the modern water table. But the Merkes area in the city's midst has produced a number of houses of the period, some graves, and what may be traces of pottery kilns. The Kassite administrative capital Dur-Kurigalzu offers more substantial remains, as do some of the cities which first rose to prominence in the Sumerian Early Dynastic period, like Ur, Larsa, and Nippur. The Kassite levels of these cities provide indications of the honour and respect accorded them by their Late Bronze Age rulers, no doubt because of their venerable antiquity.

The Kassites have sometimes been criticized, rather unfairly, for their conservatism and 'non-progressive' attitudes, for the 'static' nature of Babylonian society under their rule, and for the loss of their own identity through their readiness to adopt in all its aspects the civilization and traditions of the land they came to occupy and dominate. In fact, the Kassite period in Babylonian history was one of great cultural and intellectual vibrancy, no doubt largely due to the political stability that Kassite rulers bestowed upon their land, through their peaceful political unification of it, their highly efficient and well-organized bureaucratic system, and the respect they showed for the land's established traditions and customs. They embraced these enthusiastically, made them their own, and actively encouraged and promoted them. They did so to the extent that their own cultural and ethnic identity is all but totally unknown to us. Almost the only features we can attribute directly to Kassite influence are the breeding of horses and important developments in chariot technology. But beyond these specifically Kassite features, the influence of Kassite Babylonia on the broader Near Eastern world was enormous.

As we have noted, it was at this time that Babylonian became the international language of diplomacy throughout the Near East. And that brings us to the extremely important role Kassite civilization played in the history of Near Eastern literature. For it was in the Kassite period that what we now call the 'Standard Babylonian dialect' was developed, the literary dialect henceforth used throughout Mesopotamia and other parts of the Near Eastern world for the remainder of the second millennium and much of the first. The Standard Babylonian version of the Gilgamesh epic, best known from first-millennium texts, is perhaps the most striking example of this. Like many of the literary 'classics' from the Sumerian and other early civilizations, the epic owes its survival largely to the preservation, nurturing, and patronage of long-standing Mesopotamian cultural traditions by the rulers of Kassite Babylonia.

Traditional Babylonian religion too was nurtured and preserved by the Kassite regime, as illustrated by its promotion of the traditional cults, and under its sponsorship and patronage the repair and restoration of temples throughout the land. One of the noteworthy features of this age was the promotion of the worship of Marduk, who became the greatest god in the Babylonian pantheon, thus achieving superiority over Enlil, once the supreme divinity of the Mesopotamian world.

International trading activity was essential to the prosperity and development of Babylonian society, given the dearth of basic raw materials in southern Mesopotamia, especially timber and metals. In the Kassite period, trading connections extended to Afghanistan (and perhaps to India) in the east, to the Aegean region in the west, and to Egypt in the south-west. There were also strong trading links with Babylonia's northern neighbour Assyria, especially in the fourteenth and thirteenth centuries, despite the periods of hostility and conflict between them. Luxury goods too were imported into Babylonia, including precious and semi-precious stones, like carnelian and lapis lazuli, and other exotic items from perhaps as far afield as India. And we know from the Amarna letters that large quantities of gold were imported into Babylonia from Egypt. The Amarna letters consist of correspondence exchanged between the pharaoh and his international peers and subject rulers in the mid-fourteenth century BC. They were among the cache of tablets discovered in 1887 at el-Amarna (ancient Akhetaten) in Egypt.

In exchange for imported goods, the Babylonians exported a wide range of manufactured items, including textiles, and the products of highly skilled craftsmen, jewellers, and gold- and silver-smiths. Horses seem also to have been among Babylonian exports. These were in demand in foreign countries for breeding purposes as well as for use for transport in both military and non-military contexts.

Medicine was another skilled profession for which Babylonians were well known. This is illustrated by a letter from a Hittite king called Hattusili to his Babylonian royal brother Kadashman-Enlil II. The latter had complained of Hattusili's failure to return to him two doctors and an incantation priest sent from Babylonia on temporary loan to the Hittite court. In response, Hattusili informed his correspondent that the first doctor had decided to stay in the Hittite capital (he did so after receiving a substantial bribe), the incantation priest had gone missing, and the second doctor had died. Then in what appears to be an extraordinary display of chutzpah, Hattusili added that he would like some statues for his family quarters, and could his royal brother please send him a sculptor to do the job. The Babylonians had an international reputation as skilled artists as well as medical practitioners!

Chapter 5
Writing, scribes, and literature

Writing and the early historical era

The earliest known examples of writing in the Near East come from the southern Mesopotamian city Uruk. Dating to *c.*3300 BC, these first written records were simple pictograms, used to record such things as the number of livestock a person owned or the amount of grain he produced. Clay was the material universally used as the writing surface for these inscriptions, as indeed it was for the vast majority of records produced in the Near East for almost 3,000 years. But the early pictograms were quite quickly replaced by a script we now call cuneiform. It consisted of groups of wedge-shaped signs made by pressing into soft clay the triangular ends of reeds cut from the banks of the Mesopotamian and other rivers. The Sumerians were closely associated with the evolution of the written record, and by the end of the third millennium writing had become a highly sophisticated medium used for social, business, and political communications, record-keeping, and literary expression. It was one of the chief hallmarks of the first phase in the historical era of Near Eastern civilization.

By the beginning of the Old Babylonian Kingdom, the Sumerians and their civilization were but memories of a past age, and the Sumerian language was no longer a spoken one. Its place was taken by the Akkadian language. Akkadian, or more precisely the Babylonian version of it, became the predominant everyday tongue of the Old Babylonian Kingdom. But even though Sumerian was now a dead language, it acquired a revered status in educated and cultured circles in Babylonian society. Its important literary works were preserved and translated into Akkadian, like the poems about a king called Gilgamesh, ruler of Uruk.

The scribal schools

The most important institutions for the preservation of the Sumerian legacy were the Babylonian schools where young men were trained for the scribal profession. The term *edubba* was used for such institutions. While according to some scholars, basic literacy (i.e. the ability to read and write simple documents) may have been fairly common from the Old Babylonian period onwards, reading and writing skills of a more complex order, encompassing both technical and scholarly literacy, were acquired by a relatively small proportion of the Babylonian population. Mastering the sheer mechanics of literacy at its highest levels was in itself a daunting challenge, for the most developed cuneiform scripts contained over 500 syllable and concept signs, requiring a rigorous learning programme to achieve competence in them.

But the schools were not simply places for attaining a high level of reading and writing skills. Their curriculum covered a number of branches of knowledge, including maths, astronomy, grammar, music, and land-surveying—as well as a study of the revered Sumerian language. ('What kind of scribe is one who knows no Sumerian?' reads an old proverb.) Lexical texts have survived, with lists of words in Sumerian paired with their Babylonian equivalents—all to be learnt by heart. And as part of the process of learning Sumerian, students were obliged to copy and recopy the famous surviving works of Sumerian literature. We are greatly indebted to the Old Babylonian scribal schools for these lexical lists and copying exercises, for much of our knowledge of Sumerian literary tradition depends on the preservation of these texts from their original school setting. School hours were long—from sunrise to sunset—and education began at an early age and continued into early adult life. Discipline was harsh with beatings inflicted on students for incompetence, lack of application, and misbehaviour.

But the rewards for successful students could be considerable. Possessed of skills which the great majority of their fellow-countrymen lacked, and in a society where the kings themselves may have had no more than basic literacy, a scribe was a vital element in the maintenance of his society. And his profession was an almost exclusively male preserve (though we do find a few instances of female scribes). Even for males, the privilege of a scribal education was not open to all and sundry. In most if not all cases, scribes belonged to a profession which was confined to a select group of families, the privilege of training in the profession being inherited by a son from his father. There was also specialization within the scribal families, with certain family groups or clans staking a claim to particular disciplines associated with scribal activity (though this is only attested for the first millennium BC), such as exorcism and astronomy.

Once they had completed their basic education, which meant acquiring competence in reading and writing, including a knowledge of the Sumerian language, some students progressed to studies which would prepare them for a life in the palace administration. Most who followed this course would have careers as clerks in the imperial service, much like public servants in modern-day bureaucracies. But some rose to high positions in the royal administration, perhaps becoming consultants to the king himself, advising him on a range of matters including foreign policy and diplomatic relations with foreign courts. Other scribes apparently did freelance work, hiring themselves out to anyone who wanted a letter dictated or read to them.

Divination

Another prestigious option for those who had completed their basic training at a scribal school was to undertake advanced study under special senior tutors and teachers (possibly members of their own families) in such highly regarded professions as divination. Put most simply, the art of divination was the practice of using supernatural or magical means to gain knowledge about the future. Throughout Babylonian history, divination played a major role in shaping the lives, the plans, and the activities of the peoples who inhabited the Babylonian world, and indeed the ancient Near Eastern world in general. A basic principle underlying it is that the outcome of a particular event can be predicted if one knows the outcome of a similar event that happened in the past. Such knowledge enables one to provide for such an outcome, or to seek to avoid or manipulate it. This belief and the practices associated with it operated at all levels of Babylonian society, from the humblest labourer and servant to the society's most elite members, including the king himself.

Divination was not mere fortune-telling. It was regarded as one of the fundamental and most important sciences of Babylonian life, one that was practised by highly skilled professionals who were consulted on all important matters of both a public and a private nature. The consultants on matters of state had access to detailed records kept in official archives of past events and their outcomes. One of the important tasks of a particular group of scribes was to gather together all such information, updating their material as new events occurred, and to systematize and categorize the vast number of tablets containing this information for ease of reference when the need for consulting them arose.

But by its very nature, divination meant communicating with one or other of the gods. As part of the divination process, the practitioners of the profession were called upon to interpret various signs provided by the gods in connection with (for example) a particular enterprise that was being planned or a disaster that had befallen the land, like plague or drought. This was in order to secure a god's approval for the enterprise, or to determine the cause of his or her wrath which had led to the land being punished. Methods of determining the divine will varied considerably. They included the examination of animal entrails, the patterns of oil on water, the behaviour of animals, such as the flight of birds, and various celestial and terrestrial phenomena, like thunder, hail, and earthquakes.

Proactive consultation, in the form of omen-taking, such as the sacrifice of a sheep and the examination of its liver, was an important part of the process. Thus a particular celestial phenomenon or a particular type of behaviour of birds or other animals would be observed and the texts consulted to see what outcomes in the past had followed from this happening. Or if, shall we say, a king was contemplating a military campaign or a merchant a commercial operation, an animal might be sacrificed and its entrails examined to determine the likely success or failure of the mission, on the basis of what had happened on previous occasions when a similar pattern on an animal's entrails had been observed.

Scribes as creative artists

Scribes were educated not only to be copyists or clerks or advisers, albeit at the highest level of society, or interpreters of divine will. The great scholars of the Babylonian world were essentially products of the scribal training institutions, and some became important creative artists in their own right. Thus it was to an unknown scribe of the Old Babylonian period that we can attribute the first version of the Gilgamesh epic, the so-called Old Babylonian version. I shall return to this composition later in the chapter, simply pointing out here that while there were a number of Sumerian poems about Gilgamesh in existence and perhaps other such poems which were translated into the Babylonian dialect of Akkadian, the epic was a fresh new creation by a Babylonian scholar, a product of the Babylonian scribal school system.

The scribal traditions of the Old Babylonian school were carried on and further developed by the scribes of the Kassite period who played a major role in nurturing and preserving the traditions of Babylonian culture. But far from merely recopying texts of the Old Babylonian period, scholar-scribes of the Kassite period also substantially adapted and reworked many that had come down to them in Old Babylonian copies, as well as making significant new additions to the repertoire of Babylonian texts. They also expanded and organized into series many of the texts on divination and exorcism. Those who undertook these projects are referred to as Middle Babylonian scholars. To them are due what we call the Standard Versions of a number of Babylonian texts, including the Gilgamesh epic, which in this period was much expanded and altered from the original Old Babylonian version.

But Kassite scholars produced new compositions as well, contributing among other things to a genre of literature which we now call 'wisdom literature'. Compositions in this genre were concerned with a range of moral and ethical issues. Overall, the last centuries of the second millennium, including the late Kassite period, were very active ones in the history of Babylonian literature. But the old scribal schools designated by the term *edubba* seem no longer to have existed in this period. Education was now largely the preserve of a small number of aristocratic families.

The decline and demise of the cuneiform tradition

The survival of so many of the works of this period, including those copied or adapted from earlier periods, is due very largely to their preservation in the libraries of seventh-century BC Neo-Assyrian kings, most notably the great library of King Ashurbanipal in Nineveh, discovered during nineteenth-century AD excavations of the city. A century after Ashurbanipal stocked his library with texts gathered from all parts of his realm, writing in the cuneiform script was rapidly disappearing. It did survive for a number of centuries more in Babylonia, preserved in scholarly tradition, until the end of the first century AD. Inexorably, however, the cuneiform tradition gave way to Aramaic, which had a much simpler alphabetic script and had long been the international language of diplomacy. The rich world of cuneiform literature was lost completely, and along with it, the vast range of knowledge about the cuneiform-writing civilizations—until the rediscovery in the nineteenth century of the cuneiform tablet archives and the decipherment of the languages in which they were written.

A selection of Babylonian literary compositions

Let us now briefly consider some of the most important surviving examples of Babylonian literature, copied and sometimes adapted by many generations of scribes, and finally preserved for us in Ashurbanipal's library. We shall deal with three of them here, ending with the most famous of them all—the Epic of Gilgamesh.

The *Epic of Creation*, still often referred to by its opening words *Enūma eliš* ('When on high'), was probably composed (at least in its surviving form) during the Kassite period. Some 1,092 lines in length and spread over seven tablets, it is not really a poem about the world's creation, though it begins from that point. Rather, it is an account of the battle between Tiamat, primordial goddess of the ocean, supported by an army of fierce monsters whom she had created, and a new generation of gods led by Marduk. The contest is won by Marduk, who kills Tiamat, divides her body into two, and creates heaven and earth from the two parts. He then becomes the head of the Babylonian pantheon (the reward he demands and is granted by the gods for his victory), and allocates to its members specific roles and spheres of responsibility. To provide them with a labour force, he creates mankind, from the blood of the god Qingu who had incited Tiamat to go to war. As the climax of his achievements, Marduk builds the city of Babylon. The epic celebrating his deeds was performed each year, on the evening of the fourth day of the Babylonian New Year festival.

Another well-known Babylonian composition shares several features with this poem. The *Atrahasis (Atramhasis) Epic* (the name means 'Exceedingly-Wise'), 1,245 lines in length, has come down to us in its Old Babylonian form. However, its origins may date back much earlier, and many versions of it survive from a number of periods of Mesopotamian history. The story of its hero Atrahasis actually begins before human beings existed. In this primordial age, the lower-ranking gods had to do all the manual labour. When they grumbled and became rebellious, the higher gods responded by creating humankind, out of the body of one of the rebels killed in the uprising, to take over the menial, burdensome tasks formerly imposed upon the lesser gods. But the humans too became troublesome, to the point where their creators decided to wipe them out in a great flood. One of the gods, Enki, warned his mortal protégé Atrahasis about the impending destruction, and urged him to build a large boat, to save himself and his family from the catastrophe in which all other human beings would perish. The survival of the human race was thus assured.

What makes Atrahasis' story particularly interesting to us is that it contains the first known literary account of a Great Flood. The ancestor of many ancient Flood stories, its descendants include the tale told by Uta-napishtim in the Standard Babylonian version of the Gilgamesh epic, and, according to a number of scholars, the story of Noah in Old Testament tradition.

6. Gilgamesh.

The Epic of Gilgamesh occupies a venerable place in the repertoire
of world literature (Figure 6). It is one of the great ancestors of
the epic genre, whose most illustrious successors in the Classical
era were Homer's poems, the *Iliad* and the *Odyssey*, and Virgil's
masterpiece the *Aeneid*. The epic tells how Gilgamesh, a harsh
despotic ruler of the city of Uruk, abandons his city and, after a
series of adventures which end with the painful, lingering death

of his companion Enkidu, embarks on a search for the secret of eternal life. His quest leads him to a person who has achieved immortality, a man called Uta-napishtim. Uta-napishtim explains that he and his wife had everlasting life bestowed upon them by the gods when they, alone of all humankind, survived the Great Flood. But he is now a frail and wizened old man, for the gods in granting him immortality did not add to it the gift of eternal youth. Then, to demonstrate to Gilgamesh that he will never achieve immortality himself, the old man sets him the test of staying awake for just one week—a test which Gilgamesh immediately fails. Ultimately, his quest for immortality proves futile, and after more adventures he returns to his city a chastened, wiser man. Resigned to his fate that as a mortal he will one day die, he is now ready to resume his duties as king of Uruk, ruling with justice and wisdom and building a city of surpassing splendour.

The epic is a story about human frailties and aspirations, and most particularly about the inevitability of death. The poignancy of this in a Mesopotamian context is all the greater because of the belief that there is nothing to look forward to in the afterlife—a dull, gloomy place at best. This in itself is an encouragement to make the most of what we have in the present world. There are a number of sub-themes which occur throughout the poem—friendship and grief at the loss of a loved one, arrogance and the retribution which follows from it, the allurements of material pleasures that seek to divert the traveller from his goal, the corruption of innocence by the seductions of civilization, and the responsibilities that accompany the exercise of power.

Gilgamesh was almost certainly a genuine historical figure (known as Bilgamesh in the earliest texts), a king of Uruk who lived in the first half of the third millennium, when Uruk was one of the Sumerian city-states. A number of stories which describe the exploits of this king date back to the third millennium, and were probably first written down near the millennium's end. Five of them have survived. But it was not until the early second millennium that the poem we know as the epic of Gilgamesh was composed, in the Babylonian dialect of the Akkadian language. This first composition, known as 'The Old Babylonian Version', was probably about 1,000 lines long in its complete form (it now survives only in fragments found at various locations). Though it drew some of its material from a repertoire of stories about Gilgamesh, of which death, everlasting fame, and immortality are common themes, it was essentially an original composition in terms of the development of its themes, sub-themes, and characters, all of which are skilfully woven into the poem's structure. 'Freshness', 'vibrancy', and 'simplicity' are qualities frequently applied to this first version.

Ancient Mesopotamia produced a number of literary compositions which have survived to a greater or lesser extent among the overwhelmingly larger number of other, more prosaic, texts of the era. And the epic may not have been accorded a special status in the ancient world within its literary repertoire. Nonetheless, it was regularly included among the 'classical' texts which were copied and recopied over the centuries by generations of scribes from many civilizations, even if primarily to serve as training exercises for students in the scribal schools. We have noted that the Kassite rulers of Babylonia preserved numerous customs and traditions of Babylonia's past eras. The Gilgamesh epic was one of the literary beneficiaries of their policies. Copies of the poem found their way into many parts of the Near Eastern world reflecting Babylonia's increasing international diplomatic, cultural, and commercial contacts. And as the epic passed from one generation to another and from one country to another by written transmission, it was subject to constant modifications, and adaptations.

But the most profound changes came in the last centuries of the second millennium when the so-called 'Standard Version' of the epic was produced, the version best known to us today. Tradition credits a scholar called Sīn-leqe-unninni with its composition. An exorcist by profession, Sīn-leqe-unninni probably lived some time between the thirteenth and the eleventh centuries BC. The Standard Version is much more complete than its fragmentary Old Babylonian ancestor (though there are still some fairly substantial gaps in it). And in parts where enough of the Old Babylonian text survives for comparison purposes, we can see that its author heavily adapted the earlier text, though without altering the original basic story. Some passages he took over almost without change from it, and others he slightly modified. But elsewhere his composition differed markedly from the original, with a new prologue, the elimination of some episodes from it, the introduction of others, and a considerable expansion of the original composition.

In the Standard Version, the story of Gilgamesh is divided into eleven sections, one tablet for each. The long account of the flood in the eleventh tablet was probably not part of the original epic, which *may* have alluded to the flood only briefly, if at all. In its complete form, the eleven-tablet series contained an estimated 3,000 lines of verse (only about 60 per cent of which have survived), making it by far the longest composition in the Mesopotamian literary tradition. A twelfth tablet which was later added to the series does not in fact belong to it. Identified by the title 'Gilgamesh, Enkidu, and the Underworld', it is an Akkadian translation of part of a Sumerian poem which relates Enkidu's journey to the Underworld, to retrieve for Gilgamesh various objects that had fallen into it; he is kept there until his ghost is finally allowed to return to the upper world, where he provides Gilgamesh with information about the land of the dead.

Chapter 6
The long interlude: (12th century to 7th century BC)

Babylonia in a world of dramatic change

In the early twelfth century BC, the Greek and Near Eastern worlds were shaken by a series of catastrophic upheavals. Their causes are still much debated by scholars. Waves of external invaders, prolonged droughts, earthquakes, the collapse of international trade networks, or a combination of all these, are among the many theories that have been proposed. But whatever the precise nature and causes of these upheavals, they effectively brought the Bronze Age to an end. A number of major centres of Bronze Age civilization, including the kingdom of the Hittites, collapsed, and Egypt withdrew from its involvement in the Syro-Palestinian region and lost its status as a major international power.

The end of Hittite and Egyptian control over a network of vassal states west of the Euphrates resulted in profound changes in the geopolitical configuration of the regions where they were located. This happened during the centuries of the so-called Iron Age. Smaller, initially independent kingdoms now emerged, some the successors of former Bronze Age vassal states, others entirely new foundations. In northern Mesopotamia, the kingdom of Assyria was little affected by the substantial changes occurring in other parts of the Near Eastern world, and indeed for a time flourished and expanded its territories across the Euphrates. But by the end of the millennium, it too went into decline, and remained so until its resurgence in the late tenth century when the Neo-Assyrian empire began its rise to supremacy.

All this provides us with a broad context for the period of Babylonian history which spanned the centuries from the fall of the Kassite dynasty in the mid-twelfth century to the rise of the Neo-Babylonian kingdom in the late seventh. In the course of these centuries, a number of dynasties rose and fell in Babylonia, most of them weak and short-lived, reflecting the frequent ebb and occasional flow of Babylonia's political and military fortunes. This period may be seen as a kind of lengthy interlude in Babylonian history, though in terms of its material culture, the Neo-Babylonian period flows on directly from it. We shall touch only briefly on some of its main features and highlights, which stand out in an otherwise poorly documented and largely unremarkable phase of Babylonia's story.

Following the end of the Kassite dynasty, a line of rulers called the Second Dynasty of Isin held sway in Babylonia, according to the Babylonian Kinglist (which is preserved in several versions in ancient Babylonian sources). The reigns of its eleven members (not all of them seem to have been related to each other) spanned the period from about 1154 until 1027. Despite its name, most of its members seem to have ruled from Babylon. The most famous of them was the fourth, Nebuchadnezzar I (c.1126–1105), who was particularly remembered for his invasion of Elam; in the course of this enterprise, he sacked the city of Susa, and retrieved from it the statue of the god Marduk, taken as plunder by the Elamites during their invasion of Babylonia some decades earlier.

To Nebuchadnezzar's triumph we can largely attribute a revival of Babylonian nationalism. This continued into the reign of his successor-but-one (and younger brother) Marduk-nadin-ahhe (*c*.1100–1083), when there was a fresh outbreak of hostilities with Assyria. Otherwise, we know very little about the Isin dynasty's tenure of power in Babylonia. Nor do we know the circumstances which led to its replacement by one from the Sealand in Babylonia's far south. The new regime, the so-called 'Second Sealand' dynasty, had three rulers (perhaps of Kassite origin, to judge from their names) and lasted only two decades (*c*.1026–1006) before it too disappeared into oblivion. Then followed a succession of generally insignificant dynasties, beginning with the Bazi Dynasty (*c*.1005–986), which had three rulers, also of Kassite origin, and was succeeded by the so-called 'Elamite Dynasty' (*c*.985–80), which had only one king.

Environmental factors and new tribal groups

Environmental factors also played an important role in shaping Babylonia's development in this period. One in particular is worth noting. As the second millennium drew to a close, the Euphrates' main channel shifted significantly to the west. This may have had little effect in the far south, where the river's course changed only minimally. But cities and other settlements on Babylonia's northern alluvial plain probably suffered quite severely, for here the change caused a considerable shrinkage in the amount of land that could be irrigated and an increase in the salinization of the soil. The consequent decline in the region's economic productivity was accompanied by a rise in the level of impoverishment throughout the land, and a decrease in the populations of both urban centres and rural settlements.

Added to this, the kingdom suffered further serious destabilization from aggressive Aramaean tribal groups who sought constantly to expand their territories within the kingdom's borders and win control of important trade routes. Speakers of a west Semitic language called Aramaic, the Aramaeans had spread widely through the Near Eastern world from the late second millennium BC onwards. By the end of the millennium, a number of Aramaean states had been formed, particularly in areas of Mesopotamia, Syria, and eastern Anatolia. Some of their leaders were later to play an important role in Babylonia's history. But in the late tenth century, it was Assyria which once more became Babylonia's most serious threat, a threat that materialized when the Assyrian king Adad-nirari II (911–891) defeated his Babylonian counterpart Shamash-mudammiq and conquered his entire land.

We should now introduce another group of tribal peoples who were to play an increasingly prominent role in Babylonian history. In Akkadian, they were known by the term *kaldu*. From the Greek-derived word *Chaldaioi*, we call them Chaldaeans. Also speaking a west Semitic language, they probably entered Babylonia from the north-west some time in the eleventh or tenth century BC, but subsequently established settlements along the lower Euphrates and in the Sealand marshlands at the head of the Persian Gulf. They seem to have shared a number of features with the Aramaeans, though our ancient sources make a clear distinction between the two groups. These sources identify five Chaldaean tribes, the most important of which were Bit-Dakkuri, Bit-Amukani, and Bit-Yakin (Bit = 'House of').

While many of the Chaldaeans probably continued to live a nomadic or semi-nomadic lifestyle after their arrival in Babylonia, others appear to have taken quickly to an urban existence, building their own towns and cities, and becoming closely involved in Babylonian social and political life. Some of them even adopted Babylonian names. They nonetheless maintained their traditional tribal structures and distinct identity. Some became very wealthy, through income derived from large livestock enterprises and because of the excellent strategic location of many of their settlements on major trade routes. A number of their leaders became prominent in the Babylonian political scene, and several of them actually occupied the Babylonian throne for a time, as we shall see.

Assyrian overlordship

After its low point in the late tenth century, the Babylonian kingdom experienced some resurgence in its fortunes under a king called Nabu-apla-iddina, a member of what the Babylonian Kinglist calls the 'Dynasty of E', which lasted from about 979 to 732. Nabu-apla-iddina was clearly one of the most outstanding members of this dynasty. His reign, which began *c.*888, extended over thirty-three years. Once more free of Assyrian sovereignty, Babylonia in this period was a stable, prosperous land which enjoyed a great cultural renaissance.

Traditional cult centres were restored and sacred rites which had fallen into disuse were revived. In this period too Babylonia enjoyed peaceful relations with Assyria. But the peace came to an end when the Assyrian king Shamshi-Adad V (823–811) launched four campaigns against his southern neighbour, finally capturing its king Baba-aha-iddina (812) and deporting him to Assyria. A period of chaos and anarchy followed in Babylonia. But then there was another resurgence in the country's fortunes when a king called Nabonassar mounted its throne. His period of rule (747–734) is seen as the beginning of a new era in Babylonian history. This is reflected in the fact that two major historiographic texts, the *Babylonian Chronicles* and the *'Ptolemaic Canon'*, use his reign as their starting-point in their accounts of Babylonian history.

Shortly after Nabonassar's death, Babylonia was again divided by struggles between competing power groups, including the Chaldaeans—until in 729 the Assyrian king Tiglath-pileser III intervened. Overthrowing the current occupant of the Babylonian throne, a member of one of the Chaldaean tribes, Tiglath-pileser declared himself king of Babylonia, and instituted a period of 'double monarchy'. In theory, this meant that kingship in Babylonia was shared by the Assyrian king with a Babylonian appointee. In effect, Babylonia was now subject to the sway of an Assyrian overlord. It was an intolerable situation for the hitherto independent kingdom, and Assyrian sovereignty was constantly challenged, particularly by a series of Chaldaean leaders. By the eighth century, Chaldaean tribal groups had become a major political force in Babylonia, and during the course of the century three of their leaders occupied the Babylonian throne.

The most notable of them was a man called Marduk-apla-iddina, better known to us by his biblical name Merodach-baladan. Twice king of Babylonia (721–710 and 703), Merodach-baladan united the land under his leadership for a protracted struggle to free his fellow-countrymen from the Assyrian yoke. He was supported in his conflict with the Assyrian king Sargon by his allies the Elamites. As the contest played itself out, he won some significant victories, and indeed claimed to have regained his country's independence. But Assyrian determination to win back control of Babylonia eventually forced him to abandon his throne and flee for his life (710). Seven years later, he returned to the fray, reclaiming his country's kingship and stirring up resistance against the new Assyrian ruler Sennacherib, until the latter inflicted a devastating defeat on his forces in a showdown in southern Babylonia. Merodach-baladan once more fled for his life. He sought and was granted refuge in Elam, where he died soon afterwards.

Sennacherib now abolished the double monarchy (which had never effectively existed) and appointed first a Babylonian puppet and then one of his own sons to its throne. This prompted a campaign into Babylonia by the Elamite king Hallushu (or Hallushu-Inshushinak), who sought to establish his own authority there. He did in fact succeed in removing Sennacherib's son from Babylonia's throne and setting up his own appointee in his place. But his enterprise ended abruptly when Sennacherib invaded Babylonia once more, and routed the Elamite and Babylonian forces in a battle near Nippur. The Elamite king fled back to Susa, where he was assassinated by his own subjects. Sennacherib took prisoner and executed the man he had put on the Babylonian throne. The Assyrian was again master of Babylonia.

But Babylonian resistance soon broke out afresh. It was first led by another Chaldaean leader, Mushezib-Marduk, who defied the Assyrians for several years before Sennacherib launched a devastating campaign against him in 689. Babylon was destroyed in the course of it, and Mushezib-Marduk taken prisoner and deported to Assyria. Yet the spirit of independence still flared strongly in the Babylonian breast, and anti-Assyrian resistance movements continued in the reigns of Sennacherib's successors. Victory was finally achieved by a leader called Nabopolassar. In 626, he seized the throne in Babylon, and became the first of a series of kings who ruled over Babylonia during the greatest period of its history—the period of the Neo-Babylonian empire (626–539).

The preservation of Babylonian cultural traditions

During the first millennium BC, Aramaean influence spread widely through Babylonia, as indeed it did through other parts of the Near Eastern world. This is particularly evident from the increasing use of the Aramaic language as the medium of written communication, and Aramaic progressively became the international lingua franca of the Near Eastern world. Even so, the cuneiform tradition persisted in the Babylonian scribal establishments until the first century AD, as we have noted, and Babylonian cultural institutions and traditions extending back to the Old Babylonian and Kassite periods were preserved. Reverence for the kingdom's past cultural history helped ensure the survival of many of the great works of Babylonian literature and science.

Sadly, we have little material evidence of this long period of Babylonian history, between the Kassite and Neo-Babylonian eras, though some finds dating to it have come to light in Babylon and several other Babylonian cities, notably Ur. We know too that a number of Assyrian kings, especially Esarhaddon and his son and successor Ashurbanipal, were enthusiastic promoters of Babylonian culture. This is demonstrated by their extensive building and restoration projects in Babylonia, particularly in Babylon. Unfortunately, our information about these projects comes only from Assyrian written records, for the archaeological record has left us almost no tangible evidence of Assyria's contributions to the preservation of Babylonian culture. But as described in their written records, these contributions make clear how revered Babylonian culture was beyond the confines of Babylonia itself.

This is most famously evident from the vast tablet-finds of the library of Ashurbanipal at Nineveh, discovered in 1853. Ashurbanipal had copies made of all the most important texts which had originated in Babylonia, including the Epic of Gilgamesh, the Atrahasis myth, and the Babylonian Creation Epic. He ordered that texts be collected from the temples and palaces and other places throughout his realm and brought to his royal capital. His purpose was first and foremost a practical one. He wanted to gather together all those texts from all periods, in the lands he ruled, which he believed would provide him with the best advice for administering his empire. The collection he amassed was not intended primarily to be a repository of literary masterpieces. But in fact a number of the works he *did* collect, and which *did* fall into the category of useful advice for a reigning king, happened to be works of great literature as well. The most notable of these was the Epic of Gilgamesh. But they included all the important works of Babylonian literature up to Ashurbanipal's own time. For this we must be ever thankful to Ashurbanipal, for it is very largely due to him that the choicest examples of Mesopotamian literature are still available to us to study and enjoy today.

Chapter 7
The Neo-Babylonian empire: (626–539 BC)

The rise of the Neo-Babylonian dynasty

In November of the year 626, Babylon's throne was seized by a man called Nabopolassar. His origins are uncertain. Inscriptions refer to him as 'the son of a nobody', though there is some evidence to suggest that he was the son of a governor of Uruk under the former Assyrian administration, and may himself have governed the city before he led a rebellion against Assyrian rule. Nor is there any clear evidence that he was of Chaldaean stock, as once commonly believed. Nabopolassar appears to have emerged initially as a powerful leader in the Sealand region. But he had his sights firmly set on the throne of Babylon, and finally wrested it from Assyrian control.

The timing of his move on Babylon was opportune. Weakness and instability in the heartland of the Assyrian kingdom, which followed shortly after the death of Assyria's last great king Ashurbanipal, could be exploited by a vigorous new Babylonian leader to throw off the shackles of Assyrian overlordship and establish a new independent kingdom in the south. And power struggles among competing factions in Babylonia itself helped ensure that Nabopolassar faced no united opposition when he sought to impose his control upon the entire land.

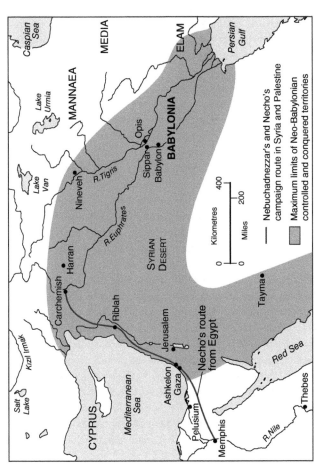

7. **Maximum extent of Neo-Babylonian controlled and conquered territories.**

Yet it took him ten years to consolidate his position on Babylon's throne, in the face of a series of attempts by Assyria to re-establish its sovereignty over its southern neighbour, and continuing political instability within Babylonia itself. After finally overcoming all obstacles, the upstart king founded a new royal dynasty. From its seat in Babylon, the rulers of this dynasty and a successor to it called Nabonidus presided over what we call the Neo-Babylonian empire (Figure 7). (As we noted earlier, however, ancient historiographers begin their account of Babylonian history with the reign of King Nabonassar (747–734), and in intellectual and cultural terms too, this is often considered a more appropriate starting-point for use of the term 'Neo-Babylonian'.)

By 616, Nabopolassar had asserted his authority in his own land to the point where he could dispose for all time of the Assyrian menace by invading his former overlord's core territories. He penetrated Assyrian territory as far north as the tradition capital Ashur, which he attacked. On this occasion, strong Assyrian resistance forced his army's withdrawal. But Assyria was now being harassed by another powerful enemy, this one from the east—the kingdom of Media in western Iran. In the year 614, the Median king Huvakshatra (Cyaxares in Herodotus) marched against and sacked both Ashur and another great Assyrian royal capital, Nimrud. It would be a good thing, Nabopolassar realized, to make an alliance with this man. And so he did, in time for their joint armies to move in for the kill, attacking and razing to the ground the last great Assyrian royal city, Nineveh. This happened in the year 612. The Neo-Assyrian empire was now effectively at an end. But in a last-ditch effort to save at least a remnant of his kingdom, the last Assyrian king, Ashur-uballit II (612–610), took refuge in the northern Mesopotamian city Harran, where he set up his court. He had but a faint hope of holding out there.

Egypt enters the fray

That brings another major player into the scene—Egypt. In 610, Egypt's throne was occupied by an enterprising new ruler, Necho II.

With aspirations for restoring Egypt to its status as a major international power, Necho made plans for the conquest of Syria and Palestine. As a first step towards this, he responded to an appeal for assistance from his Assyrian royal brother and set out for Harran, passing through Palestine and Syria on his way. But his expedition was too late to save this last remaining Assyrian stronghold. When Ashur-uballit realized that help from Egypt would come too late to save the city, he promptly abandoned it to the fast-approaching Babylonian and Median armies, who captured and sacked it.

Necho was probably not too concerned about the failure of his alleged mission. He must have realized that the Assyrian empire was doomed anyhow. Of more concern to him was that its demise left a power vacuum in Assyria's former subject territories, including those west of the Euphrates. His northern campaign gave him the opportunity to establish his own authority in these territories, most notably in Syria and Palestine. For he had no doubt that the Babylonians, fresh from their Assyrian triumphs, would quickly turn their attention westwards. His fears were justified. Very soon, and for the first time in Babylonian history, a Babylonian king sought to make himself overlord of the lands lying between the Euphrates and the Mediterranean Sea. To pre-empt this, Necho sought to consolidate his own hold over the region during his march back to Egypt through Syria and Palestine. As part of the process, he established a regional headquarters in the city of Riblah on the Orontes river. He did succeed in asserting his authority over the Syro-Palestinian regions on his homeward journey—but just for the time being. Four years later, in 605, he had to return to his northern subject territories—to confront a new challenge to his sovereignty over them.

The reign of Nebuchadnezzar

We come now to one of the most famous, and (deservedly or not) infamous figures of the ancient world, and certainly the defining figure of the Neo-Babylonian era—Nebuchadnezzar II. Strictly, we should call him 'Nebuchadrezzar'. This more accurately reflects the Akkadian form of his name—*Nabū-kudurrī-usur*, meaning 'O Nabū, protect my heir'. Both forms appear in the Old Testament, but Nebuchadnezzar is the one more commonly used there, notably in the Book of Daniel.

As crown prince, successor-in-waiting to his father Nabopolassar, Nebuchadnezzar had already become a battle-hardened warrior under his father's command. And indeed his father entrusted him with sole command of an expedition across the Euphrates in 605. It was an extremely important mission, for it would bring the prince into head-on conflict with Necho, the ultimate prize being permanent sovereignty over Syria and Palestine. The military showdown between Necho's and Nebuchadnezzar's armies took place near the city of Carchemish on the west bank of the Euphrates. Nebuchadnezzar won a resounding victory, and Necho was forced to retreat to Egypt, with what was left of his forces. Nebuchadnezzar continued his operations in the west, consolidating his hold over the lands of Syria and Palestine, and was busy with these when he received word that on 8 May 605 his father had died. Hastily gathering up the spoils of his operations in the region, including Judaean, Phoenician, Syrian, and Egyptian prisoners for transportation to Babylonia, he returned to his capital, attended to the ceremonies for his father's death, and was installed on Babylon's throne as his kingdom's new ruler. The accession, we are told, took place on 1 June—just twenty-four days after his father's death.

But he had barely warmed his throne before he set out for the west once more, to make certain that his authority was firmly embedded over the resource-rich and strategically important lands beyond the Euphrates. The rulers of these lands did not hesitate to assure him that it was, acknowledging the Babylonian as their overlord and accompanying their pledges of loyalty with large quantities of tribute. To keep a check on their continuing loyalty, Nebuchadnezzar made regular tours of inspection through their lands for the next ten years. But his regular appearances in his western territories had another purpose as well. There was the matter of a possible future challenge from Egypt to be considered.

Necho had by no means given up his ambitions to regain control of the lands to his north, and indeed word reached Nebuchadnezzar that he was mustering his forces for a fresh campaign there. This was in the year 601. Reinforcing his Babylonian garrisons stationed in Syria and Palestine, Nebuchadnezzar decided to pre-empt an Egyptian invasion by marching south to confront the Egyptian army before it advanced into Babylonian-controlled territory. The two armies met near the city of Pelusium, which lay at the north-eastern end of the Egyptian Delta; it was on the route from Egypt to Gaza. Both sides sustained heavy casualties in the conflict. Nebuchadnezzar had to return home to rebuild his army. Necho *may* have advanced as far as Gaza. But if so, he got no further, and neither he nor any subsequent members of his dynasty, the Twenty-Sixth so-called Saite dynasty, were ever again able to establish Egyptian authority over the lands of Syria and Palestine. Ultimately, then, the battle had a successful outcome for Nebuchadnezzar.

But Nebuchadnezzar was left with an unresolved issue in his Palestinian territories. Three years before the battle at Pelusium, Jehoiakim, king of Judah, had pledged allegiance to him. But after the showdown, and believing that Necho had got the better of it, Jehoiakim switched sides to Egypt. He nonetheless remained securely on his throne for several more years before Nebuchadnezzar was ready to take action against him. This came in the year 597 when the Babylonian marched into Jehoiakim's kingdom and laid siege to Jerusalem. By now, however, there was a new king on the Judaean throne. Three months earlier Jehoiakim had died, to be replaced by his eighteen-year-old son, Jehoiachin. The fledgling ruler promptly surrendered to Nebuchadnezzar, realizing that resistance was futile, and was deported to Babylon, together with his wives and the rest of his royal entourage, according to the Old Testament account (2 Kings 24: 14–16), plus 10,000 soldiers, officers, craftsmen, and smiths.

In Jehoiachin's place Nebuchadnezzar installed a puppet ruler called Zedekiah. For more than eight years, Zedekiah remained loyal to his overlord. But finally, in his ninth year, he rebelled. An account of all this is contained in our Old Testament sources (2 Kings 24: 17–25: 1, Jer. 39: 1). The rebellion prompted a full-scale expedition by a furious Nebuchadnezzar, who laid waste the countryside around Jerusalem then placed the city under siege. After an abortive attempt by an Egyptian expeditionary force to rescue the beleaguered city and its king, Jerusalem fell. Zedekiah managed to escape the city with his army, but Nebuchadnezzar's forces caught up with them in the plains of Jericho.

Separated from his own forces, which were now in disarray, Zedekiah was captured and brought before Nebuchadnezzar in his Syrian headquarters at Riblah (formerly used as a base by Necho). Here Nebuchadnezzar punished him cruelly for his disloyalty. After his sons were dragged before him and executed, Zedekiah's eyes were put out, and he was taken in chains to Babylon. The following month, Nebuchadnezzar sent the commander of his imperial guard to Jerusalem, with orders to destroy the city. This was in the year 587 or 586. Jerusalem's destruction brought to an end the so-called First Temple Period. According to the Old Testament account, all who survived the siege and destruction of the city, along with the majority of the rest of the kingdom's population, were deported to Babylonia. Ration-lists excavated in Nebuchadnezzar's Southern Palace mention Judaean exiles, including Jehoiachin, and numerous other foreigners. Recently discovered cuneiform tablets also attest the settlement of some of the deportees in the countryside of central Babylonia. Thus began the period of the Jewish exile. It was to last almost fifty years.

Jerusalem's destruction left but one major centre of resistance to Nebuchadnezzar in the Syro-Palestine region. This was the island-city of Tyre, which had courageously held out against submission to the Babylonians. Nebuchadnezzar now placed it under siege. For thirteen years, the Jewish historian Josephus tells us, Tyre defied its attacker (586–573). Even then, Nebuchadnezzar failed to take the city by force. It finally submitted to him, no doubt exhausted by the length of the siege and the privations which its occupants must have suffered, and Babylonian rule was installed there. It was also installed in the city of Sidon, which lay to the north of Tyre.

We know little else about the historical events of Nebuchadnezzar's reign. While it seems, overall, to have been a stable period in Babylonian history, we do hear of a major rebellion that flared up in the tenth year of the king's reign (595) in his own homeland. The rebellion was suppressed, but apparently only after the slaughter of many of the king's troops who had joined the uprising. What about the Medes during this period? They had after all facilitated the rise of the Neo-Babylonian empire as Nabopolassar's partners in the destruction of the Assyrian empire. But our Babylonian records are silent about them in the decades that followed Assyria's fall. This *may* indicate that relations between the two powers remained peaceful (or relatively so) for the rest of Nabopolassar's reign and at least a large part of Nebuchadnezzar's.

Yet in what were probably the later years of his reign, Nebuchadnezzar built a great defensive wall, called the Median Wall, north of his capital—across the narrow neck of land between Sippar and Opis, where the Tigris and Euphrates closely approach each other. Circumstances unknown to us must have arisen to persuade him of the need to bolster his kingdom's heartland against attacks from the north, whether by the Medes, or by other enemy forces who threatened his northern frontier.

If we leave aside the biblical tradition which depicts
Nebuchadnezzar as one of the blackest of all villains in the Old
Testament, this second king of the Neo-Babylonian empire well
warrants a place among the outstanding rulers of the ancient Near
Eastern world. Militarily, he established the most powerful and
the most far-reaching empire of any Babylonian king, all the way
back to and including Hammurabi. And to Babylonia itself he
brought a stability which was no doubt the product of a sound
and efficient administrative system. Its success may have been
due largely to his proclaimed emphasis on justice throughout
his land. In a time-honoured Mesopotamian royal tradition,
his inscriptions declare him a 'king of justice' and record his
achievements in rooting out abuses and injustice, especially in
those cases where society's weakest and most vulnerable members
were subjected to exploitation by those who had authority
over them. We have no reason to believe that this was mere
propaganda, or that Nebuchadnezzar did not apply himself
conscientiously to the task of ensuring that the dispensation of
justice was a prime consideration in the administration of
his land.

So too in the tradition of his most illustrious royal predecessors,
he prided himself on being a great builder. And he justified this
pride by vigorously setting about the task of constructing new
temples throughout his land, and restoring those that had fallen
into disrepair. The king's royal capital Babylon above all benefited
from his new building projects. These included restoration of the
main temple precinct, Esangila, containing the cult centre of
Babylonia's chief deity Marduk, and extensive other building
works, including a complex series of walls designed to protect the
capital against flooding as well as keeping out its enemies.

Of course, many of these enterprises must have been financed by
the spoils of military campaigns. Prisoners were part of the spoils,
and Judaea was far from being the only land from which large
numbers of the conquered population were deported to Babylonia

and used as labour forces on Nebuchadnezzar's building projects. But it was as a builder rather than a warrior that Nebuchadnezzar should best be remembered—and that is how he wanted to be remembered, as many of his inscriptions make clear. This is related to the Babylonian ideology of kingship. His reign too saw a vigorous promotion of the arts and sciences, for which the Kassite kings had earlier established a reputation.

Nebuchadnezzar's first successors

The years following Nebuchadnezzar's reign saw a gradual crumbling of the empire he and his father had built. On his death in 562, he was succeeded by his son Amel-Marduk (biblical Evil-Merodach; 2 Kings 25: 27, Jer. 52: 31) who reigned only two years before he was assassinated in a palace coup in 560 and replaced on the throne by a man called Nergal-sharra-usur, better known to us as Neriglissar. This man, *perhaps* his predecessor's brother-in-law (if we accept what the third-century historian-priest Berossos tells us), may well have had a part in the coup. Amel-Marduk was noted, or remembered, only for his licentious behaviour and arbitrary exercise of power. His widespread unpopularity undoubtedly proved his undoing.

Neriglissar was a rather more responsible king. Our sources record his restoration of temples both in the capital and in the city of Borsippa, and tell us of a successful campaign he conducted into the country called Pirindu in south-eastern Anatolia; it was part of the region later called Cilicia in Greek and Roman texts. Nebuchadnezzar seems also to have campaigned there in the thirteenth year of his reign (592–591), to judge from a text which refers to prisoners which he brought back from the region. But Babylon's hold of Pirindu appears to have been tenuous at best. Neriglissar died in unknown circumstances in 556, and his son and successor Labashi-Marduk had barely time to stake his claim to his father's throne before he was removed from it three months after Neriglissar's death by a military coup. The army officers who

8. Nabonidus.

instigated the coup replaced him with one of the most
controversial of all Babylonian rulers, a man called Nabu-na'id,
better known to us as Nabonidus (Figure 8).

The empire's last king

Nabonidus was the last ruler of the Neo-Babylonian empire. With
the end of his reign came the end of the empire. We know a good
deal about the reign itself, from a large number of written
sources—but there is a not a word of this king, at least not an
explicit word, in the Old Testament. This is partly for reasons that
will later become clear.

Nabonidus himself tells us in one of his inscriptions that he came to the throne, in the coup which dispatched his predecessor, as a nonentity without any aspirations for the kingship. He *may* in fact have had noble blood in his veins (it has also been suggested that he was of Aramaean origin), but he had absolutely no connection through blood-line or family links with the dynasty which his accession put to an end. In his fifties, or older, when he was proclaimed king, his elevation to royalty in the military coup that terminated Labashi-Marduk's brief reign suggests that he had made a name for himself in influential military circles, to the point where the troops considered him a worthy occupant of the throne.

At least to begin with, Nabonidus sought to project the image of a king who would maintain the time-honoured traditions of Babylonian royalty, giving particular attention to building programmes throughout his land, including the repair and restoration of religious sanctuaries. His strong interest in history and antiquities provided part of the context for his restoration projects. Yet he also turned his attention to military activities very soon after mounting the throne, demonstrating his credibility as a warrior-king with two successful campaigns into Hume in south-eastern Anatolia shortly after his accession. Like its neighbour Pirindu, Hume was part of the region later called Cilicia. Nebuchadnezzar had also claimed conquests there. By and large, Nabonidus's military policies seem to have been soundly based, even if they ultimately failed to save the empire from its fall.

Let us now introduce another major player in this last phase of the Neo-Babylonian empire—the king's mother, Adad-guppi. A great deal is known about this *éminence grise* from her biography, which turned up in 1956, inscribed on a stele found in the Great Mosque in the city of Harran. From this fascinating document, we learn that Adad-guppi lived to the ripe old age of 102. The enormous influence she exercised over her son led him on a course of action that provoked resentment among some of his subjects. From the final years of the Neo-Assyrian empire, Adad-guppi had been a loyal devotee of the moon god Sin and worshipped him in his great sanctuary in Harran. This city, we recall, had become the refuge of the last Assyrian king before it was destroyed by the Median–Babylonian alliance in 610. We are told in Adad-guppi's biography that after angrily abandoning the city, Sin returned to Nabonidus's mother in a dream, in response to her unwavering devotion to him, and told her that her son would have kingship bestowed upon him so that he could restore Harran and rebuild the god's temple there, the Ehulhul.

Nabonidus took to heart the message conveyed via his mother's dream, and with great enthusiasm set about the task of restoring Harran and Sin's temple. But his attention to Sin's affairs was the cause of some hostility towards him, especially among the priestly class, for he was seen to be neglecting the traditional gods, including Marduk, the most revered of them all. It was to Marduk that his first obligations were due. And it was Marduk, his subjects believed, who was really responsible for his elevation to kingship. Indeed, one of Nabonidus's inscriptions, carved on a stele found in Harran, tells us that the king's increasing devotion to Sin, at the expense of Marduk, caused unrest in many parts of his kingdom. But scholars now believe that claims once made of widespread and fierce resistance to the king on religious issues have been considerably overstated. It was also once argued that a seriously deteriorating economic situation in the country was a further cause for hostility towards Nabonidus. In fact our sources indicate that both socially and economically Babylonia prospered throughout his reign, right up to its end in 539—and well beyond it.

Nabonidus is best remembered for an extraordinary move he made early in his regnal career—one which was to have a substantial impact on his kingdom for the rest of his reign. A Babylonian Chronicle informs us that in his third year the king set out with his army for a military expedition to the west, to put down rebellions in the regions of what are now Lebanon and Transjordan. From there he took his army into northern Arabia. And here, in the summer of 552, he established a royal residence in the oasis city of Tayma (Taima, Teima)—where he remained for the next ten years, between 552 and 543. In his absence, he appointed his son Bel-shar-usur (better known to us as the biblical Belshazzar) as regent, to manage the affairs of the kingdom. Belshazzar seems to have been a conscientious stand-in for his father, maintaining the important traditional practices of Babylonian royalty and firmly supporting the cult of Marduk.

The possible reasons for Nabonidus's move to Tayma and lengthy stay there have been much debated by scholars. Was the king's apparent devotion to the god Sin the primary reason for his leaving Babylon and taking up residence in Tayma? The Babylonian scholar Marc Van De Mieroop warns us not to be too hasty in drawing this conclusion. He points out that while the cult of the moon god was indeed prominent in Arabia, there is no clear indication in Nabonidus's inscriptions that the king promoted it there. He suggests that the expansionist aims of the newly emerging Persian empire under its king Cyrus II, commonly known as Cyrus the Great, were probably more important than religious motives in Nabonidus's decision to move his court to Tayma; Cyrus's ambitions put at risk Babylon's subject territories in northern Mesopotamia and Syria, 'and the loss of these territories would have cut off Babylonia from the Mediterranean. Nabonidus may have explored new routes through the desert from Babylon to the west to secure access to that sea.'

Related to this is the suggestion that Nabonidus's actions were prompted, in part at least, by specific commercial considerations. Northern Arabia was an extremely wealthy region, through which passed strategically valuable trade routes that were used as a conduit for such merchandise as gold, frankincense, and various exotic spices. Joan Oates observes that at Tayma caravan routes from Damascus, Sheba, the Arabian Gulf, and Egypt converged: 'the city was a natural centre for Arabian trade, and the acquisition of a new trading empire in southern Arabia would have been a great achievement worthy of Nebuchadnezzar.'

Sound, practical reasons may have underpinned Nabonidus's sojourn in Tayma. But why did he stay there so long? Once he had established Babylonian authority over it, couldn't he have left it in the hands of a deputy, with the support of a strong military garrison? As the years passed, his return to his capital became a matter of increasing urgency—partly because during his absence the great New Year Festival which featured the god Marduk could not be celebrated. It was thus neglected for ten years. But there was another pressing matter requiring his presence back home—the need to restabilize his kingdom in the face of the mounting threats from beyond its frontiers.

Cyrus presented the most formidable of these threats. And it may well be that a primary motive for Nabonidus's return to his capital in 543 was to make preparations for countering a Persian invasion—not merely of his subject territories, but of the very heartland of his kingdom. Already Cyrus had demonstrated his expansionist ambitions by his campaign into western Anatolia, where he destroyed the Lydian empire in 546. And by 543 he was indeed seeking to extend his sovereignty over the lands of Mesopotamia. Realizing that invasion of his kingdom was imminent, Nabonidus ordered that the statues of all the Babylonian deities from the major temples in his land be brought to Babylon for safekeeping. That they would now be secure from the enemy was wishful thinking. The royal capital itself was soon to fall.

Well aware that Nabonidus's kingdom was almost his for the taking, Cyrus marched to the Tigris river in 539, accompanied by a Babylonian governor who had defected to the Persian side. After winning a fierce battle against Nabonidus's forces outside the city of Opis, Cyrus crossed the river and took control of the northern Babylonian city Sippar—and then Babylon itself, on 29 October 539. Both Sippar and Babylon probably surrendered without resistance. Indeed, though Cyrus had demonstrated his military might by his victory over the Babylonian forces at Opis, he also used propaganda as an effective tool in winning over the Babylonian people. Marduk himself, he claimed, had ordered him to take control of Babylon. And he consolidated his goodwill among the conquered Babylonians by ordering that the temples of Babylon and those throughout the Babylonian land be left undisturbed.

What happened to Nabonidus? He was captured by Cyrus, but his eventual fate remains uncertain. One account has him executed by his conqueror, but another tells us that Cyrus removed him from Babylon and set him up elsewhere in his realm, perhaps as a local governor.

Indeed, according to yet another source, he may have outlived Cyrus and his successor Cambyses.

Babylon's kings in biblical tradition

Surprisingly, it may seem, there is not a single reference to Nabonidus in our biblical sources. The commonly accepted explanation for this is that the writers of the relevant Old Testament books, particularly the Book of Daniel, conflated Nabonidus with Nebuchadnezzar. (The Jewish historian Josephus wrongly concluded that Belshazzar and Nabonidus were the same person.) In so doing, they blended into Nebuchadnezzar's reign a number of distorted aspects of Nabonidus's reign. Thus Nebuchadnezzar's obsession with his dreams and their correct interpretation (as related in the Book of Daniel) is seen as a reflection of Nabonidus's habit of describing his dreams in his inscriptions.

More specifically, Nabonidus's ten-year sojourn in the Arabian desert is transformed in biblical tradition into Nebuchadnezzar's seven years of madness; these years Nebuchadnezzar spent in the wilderness at God's command (as punishment for his arrogance and the pride he took in his capital), living among wild animals and eating grass, his hair growing like an eagle's feathers and his nails like a bird's claws (Daniel 4: 28–33). This lurid image is preserved in later tradition by William Blake's famous painting (Figure 9). Indeed, the biblical account of Nebuchadnezzar shaped all later perceptions of this king—at least until the decipherment of the Near Eastern languages in the nineteenth century. The discovery and translation of the cuneiform texts relating to Nebuchadnezzar's reign provided a more accurate, more balanced view of him, highlighting as they do his many positive achievements, material and social, cultural and political.

In the Book of Daniel, Nebuchadnezzar finally repents his sins and submits to God, and his sanity, throne, and kingdom are restored

9. William Blake's Nebuchadnezzar.

to him. But then comes the reign of his son, called Belshazzar in the biblical story. And it is in *his* reign that the Babylonian kingdom comes to an abrupt and violent end. The episode of the writing on the wall which appears in Belshazzar's banqueting hall when he is entertaining a thousand of his nobles has been immortalized in later tradition, most notably by Rembrandt's famous painting (Figure 10). The words MENE, MENE, TEKEL, UPHARSIN, signifying monetary values in descending order, thus a shrinking economy, were interpreted by Daniel, who declared that they indicated the imminent death of Belshazzar and the Persian conquest of his kingdom: 'God has numbered the days of your reign and brought it to an end. You have been weighed on the scales and found wanting. Your kingdom is divided and given to the Medes and Persians' (Daniel 5: 26–8).

We might at this point mention that according to the biblical account Daniel was one of a group of young men from the Israelite

10. **Belshazzar sees the 'writing on the wall', by Rembrandt.**

nobility who were 'without any physical defect, handsome, showing aptitude for every kind of learning, well informed, quick to understand, and qualified to serve in the king's palace' (Daniel 1: 3–4). (Daniel is renamed Belteshazzar by the Babylonian officials.) There can be no doubt that this biblical statement reflects a general policy which Nebuchadnezzar implemented of identifying among those deportees brought to his kingdom persons who showed particular qualities and aptitudes, training them as appropriate, and putting their skills to good effect in the cultural, intellectual, and political development of his kingdom. Persons of talent could almost certainly be assured of a good living, and advancement, in the land of their conquerors.

The writers of the Book of Daniel, probably compiled during the third and second centuries BC, were almost certainly well acquainted with the history of the Neo-Babylonian empire. They knew that Belshazzar was not the son of Nebuchadnezzar, but of the last Babylonian king, Nabonidus. And they knew too that Belshazzar was never king in his own right. Though he exercised many of the duties and responsibilities of kingship during his father's absence, he is never referred to in inscriptions of the time as any more than 'the son of the king'. And he stepped aside when his father returned to Babylon to resume full powers of kingship.

What the writers of Daniel have done is to adapt substantially the history of the Neo-Babylonian kingdom, so that they reduced Nebuchadnezzar's successors from four to one (and *that* one, Belshazzar, never a king in his own right). In so doing, their intention was to make their story as simple as possible, by removing from it the clutter of short-lived and mostly undistinguished rulers, thereby helping to make the message they sought to convey the more powerful. Nebuchadnezzar was the arch-fiend, responsible for the destruction of Jerusalem and the mass deportation of its citizens. It was important to emphasize that in carrying out these atrocities, he did so with God's consent; God sought to punish his people for their sins and wickedness, and Nebuchadnezzar was his tool. Then came God's final vengeance on the land of Babylon, the Persians now acting as the instrument of his wrath in destroying the evil empire, and its last king, Nebuchadnezzar's 'son and successor'. Belshazzar's final outrage, in the biblical story, was his act of sacrilege when he used as drinking cups for his feast sacred vessels taken by his father from the temple in Jerusalem when the city was sacked.

Chapter 8
Nebuchadnezzar's Babylon

Is not this the great Babylon I have built as the royal residence,
by my mighty power and for the glory of my majesty?

(Daniel 4: 30)

Recreating Nebuchadnezzar's royal capital

By the end of Nebuchadnezzar's reign, Babylon had become the greatest city on earth (Figure 11). The king's father and royal predecessor Nabopolassar had begun afresh the task of restoring the cities throughout his realm after destroying their former overlord Assyria. His role as a great builder, and as the sponsor and restorer of Babylonia's age-old traditions and customs—especially its time-honoured religious practices, the gods whom they honoured, and the sanctuaries and cult centres where they were performed—took pride of place among the achievements he claimed. And the son followed enthusiastically in the father's footsteps. Under Nebuchadnezzar, Babylon reached the height of its cultural, intellectual, and material splendour. And other cities of the kingdom benefited greatly during his reign, especially in their material development. Enormous resources in manpower, wealth, and building materials were required for the massive construction projects undertaken in Babylonia's cities. To a large extent, these came from the spoils of Nabopolassar's and Nebuchadnezzar's military enterprises, gathered in the aftermath

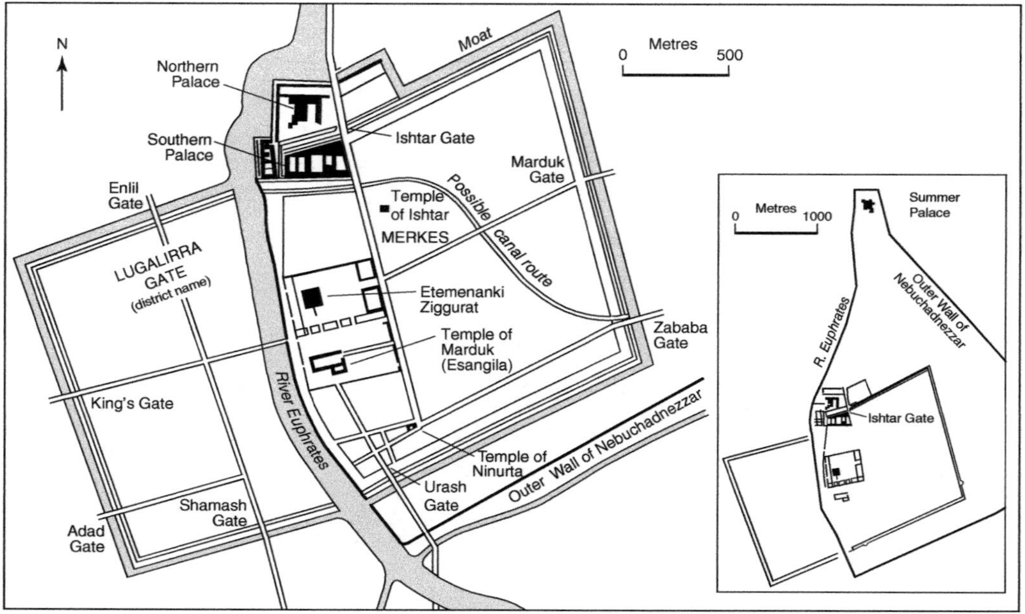
N
Northern Palace
Southern Palace
Ishtar Gate
Moat
Metres
0
500
Marduk Gate
Enlil Gate
Temple of Ishtar
MERKES
Possible canal route
LUGALIRRA GATE (district name)
Etemenanki Ziggurat
Temple of Marduk (Esangila)
Zababa Gate
King's Gate
River Euphrates
Temple of Ninurta
Outer Wall of Nebuchadnezzar
Urash Gate
Shamash Gate
Adad Gate
Metres
0
1000
Summer Palace
Outer Wall of Nebuchadnezzar
R. Euphrates
Ishtar Gate

11. Nebuchadnezzar's Babylon.

of their battlefield victories from all parts of the newly conquered lands.

Archaeology provides us with relatively detailed information about Babylon itself in this, its most splendid phase. The Neo-Babylonian city is the best preserved of all its levels, as demonstrated by Robert Koldewey's excavations, and subsequently, from 1958 onwards, by those undertaken by the Iraq Directorate-General of Antiquities. Surviving contemporary cuneiform records also provide us with a great deal of information about Nebuchadnezzar's capital. Further information (though often less reliable) comes from the accounts and descriptions of later Greek and Roman writers.

The most instructive of our Classical sources is the Greek historian Herodotus. Writing in the fifth century BC—a hundred years or so after Nebuchadnezzar's death—Herodotus has left us a relatively extensive description of Babylon *in his own time*. It's important to stress these last four words, for by then the Neo-Babylonian kingdom had fallen and Babylonia was subject to Persian control. We should also add that Herodotus himself may never have visited Babylon, relying instead on reports from those who had. There is no doubt too that some of his descriptions of the city's wonders are grossly exaggerated and quite inconsistent with what the archaeologist's spade has unearthed. Nonetheless, his description of Babylon figures largely in most accounts of Nebuchadnezzar's Babylon, and was very influential in its own and in later Classical times in forming perceptions of what the city was like at the height of its glory.

But the archaeological record is our most reliable source of information on Nebuchadnezzar's Babylon. From the excavated remains, we learn that at this time the royal capital covered some 450 hectares (850 hectares if we include the area contained within the outer defensive wall to the east). Through it flowed the Euphrates, dividing the city into two unequal portions, the larger located on the river's east bank. The two sectors of the city were linked by a bridge, supported on boat-shaped piers. You had to pay a toll to cross the bridge, but you could also cross by ferry. The river itself had its banks strengthened against erosion and floods by huge barriers of baked brick. A network of canals distributed water throughout the city.

Among the building projects begun by Nabopolassar and completed by Nebuchadnezzar were the city's massive walls, whose origins actually date back to the Neo-Assyrian period or earlier. There were two main sets of walls, an exterior wall and an inner double one. The exterior wall, extending some 18 kilometres, enclosed the part of the city that lay east of the Euphrates, and included in the far north Nebuchadnezzar's so-called 'Summer Palace'. Its defences against enemy attack were strengthened by a moat, whose waters were channelled from the Euphrates, and a rampart which extended along its entire length.

The roughly rectangular inner double-wall, with inner and outer components, extended just over 8 kilometres, and enclosed the city's main buildings. It too was further protected by a Euphrates-fed moat. The wall was surmounted by a road wide enough, according to Herodotus, to enable the passage of four-horse chariots along it, between two rows of one-roomed buildings which topped it on either side. (The first-century BC Greek historian Diodorus Siculus says that two four-horse chariots could easily pass each other on the wall.) Herodotus further claims that the fortifications were pierced by no fewer than one hundred gates! Overall, his statistics are highly inflated ones, as later Classical writers realized. But there is no doubt that the walls were an extremely impressive feature of Nebuchadnezzar's Babylon—and were ranked by some ancient writers among the Seven Wonders of the Ancient World.

Entry to Babylon through these walls was provided by a total of perhaps nine gates. Only some of these have been excavated, though we know from cuneiform records what each was called;

12. Reconstruction of the Ishtar Gate, Babylon.

they were named after gods—for example, Adad, Shamash, Enlil, and Marduk. The most famous of the Gates is the one dedicated to the goddess Ishtar (Figure 12). Originally rising to a height of 15 metres, it was decorated with blue-glazed dragon figures and animal reliefs. A partial reconstruction of the gate can be seen in the Vorderasiatische Museum in Berlin. It was this gate that gave access to the 250-metre-long Processional Way, one of the great defining features of the city and a major part of the setting for the annual New Year festival.

The New Year festival

For this twelve-day celebration, called the Akitu festival (the most important of many festivals held annually in Babylon and other Babylonian cities), statues of the chief deities of the realm were gathered together to celebrate the arrival of spring and to participate in a ritual re-enactment of the triumph of Marduk over the forces of evil. On the festival's fifth day, the statue of the god Nabu, son of Marduk, arrived by boat after a journey along the Euphrates from his city Borsippa, accompanied by the statues of other major deities from other cities, all in specially made sailing vessels decorated with precious stones.

Their destination reached, the gods were carried in procession, followed by the king and his subjects, to the temple precinct called Esangila, where Marduk was in residence. The king entered the temple's innermost sanctuary. He was stripped of all his insignia of office, and had his ears pulled and his face slapped. After this ritual humiliation, he bowed down before Marduk and assured the god that during the past year he had committed no offence nor had he neglected his religious duties or his obligations to his city. Once more, he had his face slapped, sharply enough to bring tears to his eyes (thus winning the god's approval), and then his royal insignia were restored to him.

The following day, Marduk left the temple precinct. His freshly acquired power and authority were celebrated in a huge public procession. At its head were the king and Marduk's statue, the king 'taking the god by the hand', and other deities following. There was much feasting and singing and dancing, with a great part of the population of Babylon turning out for the occasion. The procession passed along the Processional Way through the Ishtar Gate, and then proceeded along the Euphrates to the temple called the House of Akitu. Here, further ceremonies took place until the festival's eleventh day, on which the gods returned once more to Babylon. The celebration of the land's and its chief god's renewal was almost done. It ended with a great banquet, after which the other gods of the land were escorted back to their own cities in their bejewelled water-taxis.

The palaces and temples

Royal residences were constructed in many parts of the king's realm, but those of Nebuchadnezzar's Babylon dominated all others. Already his father had built an impressive palace adjacent to the Processional Way on its western side, the so-called Southern

Palace. It was rebuilt on a grander scale by Nebuchadnezzar and in its final form encompassed five courtyards, so we learn from the excavations, and many apartments and reception rooms. The grandest of the courtyards gave access to Nebuchadnezzar's throne-room. Comparable in size to the Gallery of Mirrors at Versailles, it's been suggested that this was the setting for Belshazzar's feast. The Southern Palace was the most important of Nebuchadnezzar's royal residences in Babylon, but towards the end of his reign he built a second palace immediately to its north. The theory that this palace may have contained a museum, because of the discovery there of a large number of antiquities, including a basalt lion and statues and steles of various gods, kings, and governors, some of which date back to the third millennium, has been comprehensively debunked. Both palaces were defended by huge fortification systems.

There was also a third palace in Babylon, built by Nebuchadnezzar at the extreme northern end of the city, just inside the city's exterior wall. It has been dubbed the 'Summer Palace' because in it were discovered the remains of what were once thought to be ventilation shafts; but they have turned out to be much later—part of the substructure of a fort built on the site in the Parthian era. In any case the 'Summer Palace', remote from the city's centre but still within its outer fortifications, may have provided the king with a retreat beyond the bustle of the city, while still close enough to its centre for him to be kept closely in touch with the capital's and the kingdom's affairs.

The very heart of the city was occupied by the most important sacred precinct in the Babylonian world. This was the temple enclosure called Esangila, a Sumerian name meaning 'House Whose Top is High'. Dating back at least to the early second millennium, the sanctuary had long been venerated as a place of great holiness. It contained the shrine of Babylonia's most important deity, Marduk. Destroyed by Sennacherib during his sack of Babylon in 689, it was partly rebuilt by later Assyrian kings, and the statue of Marduk, carried off by Sennacherib, was restored. However, Nebuchadnezzar ordered a total reconstruction of the precinct, with 9-metre-high gateways, cult-rooms embellished with precious metals, and doors and ceiling beams made of cedar-wood from Lebanon. The precinct also contained shrines to other important Babylonian deities, including Marduk's wife Zarpanitu and his son Nabu, the patron god of scribes. (This is a clear indication of the importance of the scribal craft, given that its patron was one of Babylonia's chief deities.) Nebuchadnezzar in one of his inscriptions tells us that the shrine of Marduk, which he ordered to be covered in gold, shone like the sun.

Within Babylon's principal cultic region, and just north of the Esangila, was Babylon's second most important cultic precinct—the sanctuary of Etemenanki, 'House of the Foundation Platform of Heaven and Earth'. Here was located the ziggurat dedicated to Marduk. The shrine of the god lay atop a six-stepped platform, perhaps first built during the late second millennium, perhaps earlier. It too had been destroyed by Sennacherib and partly restored by his successors. But, like the Esangila, its major rebuilding was due to Nebuchadnezzar after earlier reconstruction on it by his father. From this structure originated the famous biblical tradition of the 'tower of Babel'.

The two temple precincts dominated Babylon's religious life and were defining features of the city landscape. The ziggurat in particular was a prominent landmark, and perhaps provided a useful lookout point, to give early warning of an approaching enemy. But there were also many other temples located in various parts of the city, like temples of the god Shamash and the goddess Gula. These were more intimately integrated into the urban fabric; they lacked enclosing precincts but simply nestled within areas of residential housing.

As in earlier periods, the residential areas were for the most part probably linked by narrow, rambling, and sometimes dead-end streets. And, as also in the past, the houses themselves were closed off by walls from the outside world, their rooms built around a central courtyard which provided an important source of light and ventilation. The most prosperous of them sometimes had one or more additional courtyards, and very occasionally a second storey.

The 'Hanging Gardens of Babylon'

Of course, we cannot leave Nebuchadnezzar's Babylon without saying something of one of the most famous and most controversial monuments associated with it in later tradition—the so-called Hanging Gardens.

The story is a romantic one. It is told by the third-century BC Babylonian priest Berossos, who wrote (in Greek) an account of Babylonian history and traditions. Unfortunately, only fragments of his work survive. This particular story is preserved from his writings by Josephus. It relates that Nebuchadnezzar's wife, the Median princess Amyitis, pined for the lush mountain scenery of her native homeland (which contrasted strikingly with the flat, featureless landscape of Babylonia). So the king attempted to recreate for her as best he could something of her homeland environment, by setting up high stone terraces planted with all kinds of trees. In this way, he hoped, she would be forever reminded of the thickly wooded mountains of the land of her birth, and thus feel more at home in her new environment. The gardens were a labour of love for a homesick foreign bride.

The palace where Berossos alleges they were built can readily be identified with Nebuchadnezzar's Northern Palace. Yet neither here nor in the adjacent Southern Palace nor anywhere else in Babylon have any remains been found that can be proven to be those of the Hanging Gardens. Indeed, though they have long been established as one of the canonical seven wonders of the world, they alone of these wonders have yet to demonstrate that they ever existed. Robert Koldewey's belief that he had found them turned out to be baseless, and various other proposals for a location in Babylon have all been rejected. To this we must add the fact that not a single cuneiform text, belonging to Nebuchadnezzar's era or later, refers to them. Significantly, the Greek historian Herodotus, who waxes eloquent about the wonders of Babylon, has not a word to say about anything that might represent them.

We should also note that almost none of the Classical sources that refer to the Hanging Gardens assign them to Nebuchadnezzar. In one tradition, construction of them is attributed to the legendary queen Semiramis of Greek tradition, whose historical prototype was a ninth-century queen of Assyria. But Semiramis has been credited with many great monuments in Near Eastern history, especially at sites on the Euphrates and in Iran. Diodorus Siculus states that the Gardens were built not by Semiramis but by a later Syrian (probably he means 'Assyrian') king, at the request of one of his concubines, who was of Persian origin and longed for something to remind her of the mountain meadows of her homeland. Thus he created a planted garden built on ascending terraces, the weight of which was supported by a series of galleries or vaults.

Though Diodorus's account has some features in common with that of Berossos, the overall inconsistencies in our Classical sources inevitably raise doubts about whether there is any historical basis to the Hanging Gardens tradition, let alone whether the tradition can be assigned to Nebuchadnezzar's Babylon. So should we dismiss the whole notion of them as mere fantasy? Were they no more than some sort of romanticized concept of an exotic Near Eastern horticultural showpiece? That has indeed been suggested in numerous debates about the tradition.

But the view that the tradition is based on historical fact continues to resurface. Most recently, Stephanie Dalley has presented a detailed defence of it. She maintains that the Gardens did exist, but not in Babylon. Noting that on a number of occasions our Classical sources appear to confuse Babylon with the Assyrian royal capital Nineveh (and also that cities other than Babylon proper could be called 'Babylon'), Dalley has argued that the Hanging Gardens belonged to Nineveh.

Part of the support she adduces for this is a seventh-century Assyrian inscription which describes a building in Nineveh corresponding in significant respects with descriptions of the Hanging Gardens in the later Classical sources. She also draws attention to a relief sculpture, unearthed during excavations in Nineveh in 1854, depicting rows of trees planted on a series of terraces rising one above the other. This 'garden', Dalley concludes, was built by the Assyrian king Sennacherib in the century before Nebuchadnezzar became king in Babylon, and was deliberately intended by its builder to become one of the Wonders of the World.

That leaves the question of how the 'Hanging Gardens' were irrigated. Dalley believes that this was made possible when Sennacherib adopted a new method of casting bronze and used it for the production of a giant screw which could raise water in a non-stop operation from river level, and in considerable volume, to all the levels on which the garden was laid out.

In the absence of hard evidence, the 'Ninevite proposal' remains a highly speculative one. Doubts have been expressed by a number of scholars about whether the Assyrians had the technology for building a screw on the gigantic scale required for the task of providing adequate irrigation for the suspended forest. Most importantly, evidence has yet to be found in Nineveh of remains that could possibly be identified as Sennacherib's Hanging Gardens. One wonders whether there will ever be an opportunity for exploring that possibility further.

Chapter 9
Babylonia in later ages: (6th century BC to 2nd century AD)

Babylonia under Persian rule

Isaiah's prophecy about the fate of Babylon could not have been more grim: 'Babylon, the jewel of kingdoms, the glory of the Babylonians' pride, will be overthrown by God like Sodom and Gomorrah. She will never be inhabited or lived in through all generations, no Arab will pitch his tent there, no shepherd will rest his flocks there. But desert creatures will lie there, jackals will fill her houses; there the owls will dwell, and there the wild goats will leap about. Hyenas will howl in her strongholds, jackals in her luxurious palaces. Her time is at hand, and her days will not be prolonged' (Isaiah 13: 19–22). In biblical tradition, this was the apocalyptic finale of the story of Babylon—whose imminent end is announced in the writing on the wall of Belshazzar's banqueting hall, its enigmatic message foretelling Belshazzar's death and the 'Median' (i.e. Persian) seizure of his kingdom that very night.

Yet these biblical reports of Babylon's demise were greatly exaggerated. After Cyrus had invaded Babylonia in the autumn of 539, and swiftly routed Nabonidus's forces in a battle near the city of Opis, all Babylonian resistance effectively came to an end. The culminating point for Cyrus was his triumphal entry into Babylon itself, allegedly with much rejoicing. This we learn from a famous Babylonian inscription, which informs us that all the inhabitants

13. The Cyrus Cylinder.

of Babylon, and indeed the whole land of Babylonia, including kings and princes, bowed before the Persian as he came into their midst and kissed his feet, praising his name, and joyously welcoming him as their new lord. Written on a clay cylinder, commonly referred to as the Cyrus Cylinder, the inscription which provides this information was discovered in Babylon in 1879 and is now in the British Museum (Figure 13). Though its author is unknown, the text is very likely a Persian-inspired one, with an almost biblical messianic flavour. Nabonidus is singled out for particular vitriolic abuse in this and other compositions by local supporters of Cyrus.

Cyrus may not have been as enthusiastically received in the Babylonian capital—nor Nabonidus anywhere near as unpopular—as these texts make out, and the city had been carefully secured by Cyrus's troops before he ventured into it, even if no actual military action took place (which we cannot be completely sure about). Still, he may quickly have won over many of his new subjects, especially since on his entry into Babylon he gave strict orders that no harm was to be done to the city—no looting, no destruction of its buildings, no slaughter of its citizens. Indeed, he made clear from the outset that Babylon's and Babylonia's time-honoured traditions, cults, gods, and religious customs were to be honoured, preserved, and maintained.

As a signal example of his intentions, he ordered that all the statues removed by Nabonidus from their home cities and brought to Babylon for safekeeping, as the Persian invasion became imminent, were to be returned to their original sanctuaries. To Babylonia's chief god Marduk he proclaimed his particular devotion, and indeed represented himself as the agent chosen by Marduk to rule the world and reinstate the Babylonian traditions neglected or discarded by Nabonidus. To emphasize further that he was restoring to the Babylonians their old traditions, he sought to remove every trace of Nabonidus's reign, with orders that his name was to be erased from all monuments in the land.

And as yet another gesture of his respect for Babylonian traditions and his intention to maintain them, he appointed his son and designated successor Cambyses as his representative in the annual Babylonian New Year festival, never celebrated during Nabonidus's absence in Arabia. Cyrus himself adopted many of the titles and roles of traditional Babylonian kingship. His first capital, Susa, now surpassed Babylon as the Near Eastern world's centre of power. But Babylon retained its status as a royal capital, and the chief administrative centre of Mesopotamia, its bureaucratic system left largely undisturbed, though now under the authority of a Persian-appointed governor.

Cyrus is also treated very positively in the Old Testament, as the 'anointed of god' (Isaiah 45: 1) who released the Jews from their decades of bondage in Babylonia and allowed them to go home, to rebuild their devastated land and their temple in Jerusalem. Many Jews did in fact return to their homeland. But there were also many who decided to stay put. Indeed, for the younger generations, Babylonia *was* their homeland, one in which persons of enterprise, irrespective of their origins, could make a good living, in a range of commercial, cultural, and intellectual activities. Long after Cyrus's liberation of the Jews, a significantly large Jewish population continued to live in Babylonia, to enjoy the benefits that life there had to offer.

Under Cyrus's successor, Cambyses, Babylonia seems to have remained, overall, a stable, prosperous, and peaceful subject of the Persian empire. But there were dissenting elements. Following Cambyses' death, a couple of Babylonians claiming to be descendants of Nabonidus (each called himself Nebuchadnezzar) seized Babylon's throne with the backing of rebel Babylonian forces. Their ambitions were terminated by Cambyses' first effective successor, Darius I, who defeated their armies, took them prisoner, and executed them. Life in Babylonia resumed its apparently peaceful course. The new king maintained close personal links with Babylon by spending many of his winters there. And he made clear the importance and significance he attached to the city when he appointed his son and successor Xerxes as his representative in it, building a new palace to serve as his son's royal residence. This helped pave the way for a smooth transition to Xerxes' overlordship of Babylonia following his father's death in 486.

But unrest against Persian rule among at least some elements of the population continued to smoulder, and was perhaps further stoked up by increasingly heavy taxes imposed by Xerxes on his subjects to help fund his military ventures. (Indeed, Babylonia became one of the most highly taxed of all Persia's subject-states.) From this unrest, there emerged two local 'kings' who sought to seize the throne and win back Babylonian independence. They did so with the support of the Babylonian people, who murdered their Persian governor. But they had no more success than the ill-fated pair of 'Nebuchadnezzars' who had risen up against Xerxes' father. Once more, the uprising was crushed, the Babylonian capital taken, and Persian sovereignty reimposed over the land. Xerxes may have taken further retaliatory action against the capital, including the pillaging of Marduk's temple.

Indeed, some scholars have assumed that a lengthy siege and sack of the city which Herodotus (3.152–8) reports and attributes to Darius should be assigned to Xerxes. But the historical validity of the episode is highly questionable. And there is no indication in Herodotus' description of mid-fifth-century Babylon that the city had recently been sacked and plundered. On the contrary, it still clearly inspired feelings of awe and wonder in those who visited it, though it was now well past its heyday. It may indeed have benefited at this time from new building programmes, carried out on the orders of Xerxes' son and successor Artaxerxes I, who succeeded to the throne after his father's assassination in 465.

By and large, Babylonia remained a prosperous land under Persian rule, with a number of its cities continuing to be bustling centres of trade and commerce, and maintaining their reputation as major centres of learning. These features helped attract a stream of new settlers from many other lands. From both native and Classical sources, we learn of the great variety of nationalities represented in the capital and other Babylonian cities. Included among the crowds who thronged their thoroughfares were peoples from India, Afghanistan, and Iran in the east, Arabs and Egyptians from the south and south-west, Armenians from the north, and Syrians, Greeks, Carians, Lydians, and Phrygians from the north-west. A veritable babel of languages filled the streets of its cities. Babylonia may have been of only marginal political importance in the era of the Persian empire. But in terms of its cosmopolitanism and multiculturalism, it was now, perhaps more than ever before, one of the great international meeting-places of the Near Eastern world.

Alexander the Great and Babylon

Despite further periods of unrest in the reigns of Artaxerxes' successors, Babylonia remained under Persian control until the year 330. It was in this year that the final remnants of the Persian empire fell to Alexander the Great. Already the year before, Alexander and the Persian king Darius III had fought a decisive battle near the village of Gaugamela in northern Mesopotamia. Alexander won a resounding victory, and though Darius managed to escape the battlefield, he was later assassinated by one of his own generals. In this same year, Alexander swiftly imposed his rule upon Babylonia and entered its capital in triumph. In what seemed to be a case of history repeating itself, we are told that Babylon's new ruler was warmly welcomed by its populace, just as Cyrus, the founder of the empire now destroyed by Alexander, had allegedly been two centuries earlier.

Like Cyrus too, Alexander sought to win over his new subjects by showing respect and reverence for their time-honoured traditions, and in a more material way by undertaking to repair the city's great buildings, especially its religious ones. Work was begun on restoring the sacred precincts of Etemenanki and Esangila. And the great ziggurat was demolished (contemporary cuneiform tablets mention the work of removing the earth of the structure) in preparation for rebuilding it (though this never happened). Under Alexander, Babylon would achieve the heights of its former glory, for it was to become the capital of Alexander's newly acquired empire, embracing both the eastern and the western worlds. This was Alexander the Great's vision, so our sources inform us.

After spending a few months in Babylon, Alexander embarked on his campaigns further to the east, into the heartland of the Persian empire, and to Bactria (in Afghanistan) and India beyond. Eight years later, he returned to Babylon. This was in the spring of 323. Work now proceeded apace on the restoration of the holy precinct of Esangila. But Alexander did not intend his second visit to Babylon to be a long one, for while he was there, he made plans for an expedition to Arabia. As it turned out, he never left the city. Shortly before his departure on his new venture, he fell ill with a fever, to which he succumbed twelve days later. On 13 June 323, he died in his proposed new capital. He was only thirty-two years old. That put paid to the young man's ambitious plans for making Babylon once more a great royal capital.

Babylonia in the Seleucid and Roman periods

The years following Alexander's death were plagued with squabbles and military conflicts among his chief military officers, the so-called Diadochoi or 'heirs', over the carve-up of his recently won and still very fragile empire. At a conference held in Syria in 320, where the heirs sought to reach agreement by allocating various parts of the empire to themselves, one of Alexander's steadfast comrades-in-arms, a man called Seleukos, acquired control of the province of Babylonia. It was an appointment that would play a key role in his future career and the careers of his dynastic successors. But for a while control of it was seized by another of Alexander's heirs, the fierce, battle-scarred warrior called Antigonos Monophthalmos (the 'One-Eyed'). Babylonia and its chief city now became embroiled in bitter contests between the competing forces of Antigonos and Seleukos.

The latter won out in the long run, firmly re-establishing his authority over Babylonia when Antigonos was killed in battle (in Anatolia) while fighting a coalition force led by Seleukos and a number of the other heirs. Seleukos now had a large swathe of Syria added to the territories already under his control. He became the founder of what is known as the Seleucid empire, which extended over vast areas of the Near Eastern world. And he set an example for those who succeeded him in the dynasty he established by building throughout his empire a number of new cities. Many of them he colonized with Greeks, but at the same time his policy was that traditional customs and beliefs were to be preserved and respected in the cities and regions where they were practised, indigenous peoples were to be granted citizenship alongside Greeks in both the new and the old foundations, and non-Greek communities were to be recipients of benefactions and patronage from their Seleucid rulers, their religious rites, beliefs, and sanctuaries protected and honoured.

But his reign meant the beginning of the end for Babylon as a major centre of the Near Eastern world. Unlike Alexander, who planned to make the city his capital, Seleukos built for himself a new capital, c.90 kilometres to the north, on the Tigris river. It was called Seleukeia-on-the-Tigris. To it were attracted lots of new settlers, including many from Babylonia and Babylon itself. Despite its founder's professed intention of preserving traditional customs and practices, the progress of Greek culture inevitably took its toll on the old ways of life in Babylonia and other regions. But Babylon continued to be an important religious centre of the region (first assured by Seleukos's son and successor Antiochos I, who ordered the rebuilding of its most sacred precinct, Esangila), and was to remain so until at least the first century BC.

It also continued to be an important cultural and intellectual centre in this period. As Joan Oates observes, there seems to have been a revival of interest in cuneiform literature at this time, and the study of astronomy and astrology flourished, perhaps with Antiochos's active support and encouragement. Several of the king's successors bestowed favours upon Babylon, including gifts of land to it and to other Babylonian cities like the cult-centres Cutha and Borsippa. Indeed under the eighth Seleucid ruler, Antiochos IV (175–164), Babylon seemed set for a new lease of life, perhaps as a new eastern capital of the Seleucid empire, it has been suggested—though much of the traditional character of the city was very likely obscured by the new Greek colony Antiochos established there.

But not long after, Babylonia came under the control of another power, one that had arisen in Iran, c.247 BC. This was the kingdom of Parthia. The westward expansionist ambitions of this kingdom brought it into conflict with both the Seleucid rulers and their Roman successors in the region. From the reign of their king Mithradates I (171–138 BC), Parthia's rulers were frequently at war with their Seleucid rivals over control of Mesopotamia. Inevitably Babylon became caught up in these wars, with rule over it fluctuating between Seleucid and Parthian kings. Under the latter, Babylon was not entirely neglected, and indeed there is evidence of some building activity within the city during periods of Parthian domination. Most significantly, the Esangila continued to function as the spiritual heart of the city. Along with the traditional elements of Babylonian religious life, so too some of the traditional elements of Babylonian intellectual life survived well into the first century AD. Examples of the cuneiform script have been found, dating to this late period, though the documents in this script are by this time confined to astronomical and mathematical texts. And by the end of the century, the cuneiform system of writing had completely died out.

We have mixed reports from our Classical sources about the material state of Babylon in this period. Diodorus Siculus gives the impression that in the late first century BC Babylon was already a largely abandoned, desolate place. Its walls were still impressive—indeed he ranked them among the seven wonders of the world—but the area within them had by then been given over largely to farming; the other major buildings of the city, including the Esangila, were now in ruins. Yet a century later, the Roman writer Pliny the Elder indicates that the Esangila was still functioning. Indeed, it may have continued to function as late as the third century AD, even if much else around it was in a ruined, abandoned state. This was the condition in which, we are told, the emperor Trajan already in AD 116 found the city on his return journey from his campaigns east of the Euphrates. He visited Babylon to pay homage to Alexander, and offered sacrifice to the dead man's memory in the very room, allegedly, where Alexander had died.

The Babylonian legacy

But in the centuries that followed, Babylon never completely faded from human memory. Indeed, written records indicate that it was partly reoccupied in the ninth and tenth centuries AD, when it served as a provincial capital, whose administrative quarter was known as Babel. The city's biblical associations prompted visits to it by a number of early Jewish and Christian travellers. Of these, the first known was a rabbi from northern Spain, called Benjamin of Tudela. Attracted by the stories of Babylon in Jewish tradition, and by the knowledge of Jewish communities who still lived there, Benjamin visited Babylon and other sites in Babylonia twice, between 1160 and 1173. He became the first European to have left us an account of Babylon's ruins. This included a description of the remains of Nebuchadnezzar's palace. He also described what he believed were the remains of the tower of Babel. But these he claimed were in another Babylonian city, Borsippa.

A handful of travellers followed in Benjamin's wake over the next three centuries. No doubt one of the main reasons for their journeys was to see at first hand the fulfilment of the biblical prophecies—for the once proud capital of the Babylonian world was now a vast, derelict place, inhabited by snakes, scorpions, and other wild and venomous creatures (so these early travellers tell us). During the High Renaissance, from the sixteenth century onwards, Mesopotamia received an ever-increasing number of visitors from the west as interest in the ancient world and the antiquities that came from it steadily grew. Babylon became one of the chief focuses of interest, both because of its biblical associations and the many references to it in the works of Greek and Roman writers.

Up till then, and indeed until the first half of the nineteenth century, our knowledge of Babylon was based on three sources—the ruins of the city as reported by a succession of visitors from the tenth century onwards, the numerous biblical descriptions and prophecies about the city, and the reports of it by Classical writers. Most influential among these was the hostile treatment of the city in biblical sources. Not surprisingly, these sources were responsible for the highly negative perceptions of Babylon in Judaeo-Christian tradition, and this profoundly affected the way

Babylon was presented in western art and literature, as illustrated most famously by Bruegel's Tower of Babel, Blake's Nebuchadnezzar, and Rembrandt's Belshazzar.

The overall picture was clearly a distorted, and highly blinkered one. But up until the mid-Victorian era, it could hardly have been otherwise. Till then, the ancient Babylonians were unable to speak for themselves. That changed with the decipherment of the cuneiform scripts and languages by the middle of the nineteenth century. For the first time, we had access to the written records of the Babylonians themselves. Hitherto, what we knew about them had been confined to what other peoples said about them, often from a narrow, biased perspective, and often some centuries after the events they were describing. The cuneiform texts, along with the first comprehensive excavations at Babylon in the late nineteenth century, helped balance this perspective, recording as they do the numerous social, intellectual, and cultural contributions the Babylonians made to contemporary and later civilizations.

The Laws of Hammurabi emphasize the importance attached by their author, and many of his successors, to ensuring that justice prevailed throughout the land, and that society's most vulnerable members were afforded protection by the law and legal redress against their offenders. In this, Hammurabi was maintaining a basic principle of justice already established by several earlier Mesopotamian kings in their social reform programmes. But his collection of laws provided a basis for later legal pronouncements as well, like the Hittite compendia of laws. We also find echoes of a number of its clauses in Old Testament law, such as the provisions made for levirate marriage and the penalties prescribed for a range of sexual and other offences. The 'eye for an eye, tooth for a tooth' principle is well embedded in both Hammurabic and Old Testament legal tradition.

Because of their enforced stay in Babylon for almost half a century, many of the Jews, especially the priests and scholars among them, became steeped in the customs, traditions, and institutions of their Babylonian hosts, and many of these were absorbed within their own culture. Thus the biblical flood story told in Genesis clearly owes much to the account of a great flood in Mesopotamian literature, as illustrated by the flood stories in the Babylonian Atrahasis and Gilgamesh epics. These epics, along with other Mesopotamian 'classics', were integrated into the cultural fabric of the Near Eastern world for centuries to come. There are, for example, fragmentary versions of the Gilgamesh epic found in a number of centres of Near Eastern civilization spread over many centuries. Such Babylonian masterpieces became a standard part of the repertoire of the training programmes of those who studied for a career in the scribal profession.

More generally, the Babylonian language became firmly established, from Hammurabi's time on, as the major international language of the Near Eastern world, and indeed it became the lingua franca of this world for centuries to come, through the late Bronze and Iron Ages, and down into the first millennium BC, until its eventual replacement by Aramaic. It is ultimately from Babylonia, probably via the medium of scribes brought back from Syria in early Hittite campaigns in the region, that the Hittites adopted the cuneiform script for writing their own language. In the process, they incorporated the epic of Gilgamesh into their scribes' curriculum of study.

And the Hittites may have played some part in the transmission of cultural traditions originating in Babylonia, and Mesopotamia in general, to the western world of Greece and Rome, though it is likely that northern Syria played a much greater role. The eighth-century Greek epic poet Homer almost certainly knew the Gilgamesh epic and was inspired by episodes and ideas from it in his composition of the *Iliad* and the *Odyssey*. Scholars have pointed to many parallels between the Babylonian and the Homeric poems in their themes, individual episodes, and in the customs they describe. We might also mention in passing that the second-century AD satirist Lucian actually claimed that Homer was a Babylonian in origin, though almost certainly he said so with his tongue planted firmly in his cheek.

Throughout Babylonian history, there were major advances in a number of scientific fields. The Babylonians were well known for their healing skills, as illustrated by Hittite royal requests for the services of Babylonian medical practitioners during the Kassite period. Mathematics, based on the sexagesimal system (i.e. counting in units of sixty—which we still use today to some extent, for example in our measurement of time) ranked high among the fields of expertise in the Babylonian world. Already in the Old Babylonian period, students in the scribal schools acquired skills in such fields as algebra, quadratic and cubic equations, and geometry.

Mathematical studies in Babylonia were complemented by studies in the closely related fields of astronomy and astrology. Particularly in the three centuries that followed the death of Alexander, the period we call the Hellenistic Age, these studies had a major impact on the development of Greek science. Diviners and soothsayers were valued in the Babylonian world for their skills in interpreting the divine will and advising on the future, through various means such as the examination of a sacrificed sheep's liver and the observation of celestial phenomena. Designated by the term 'Chaldaean', these practitioners of the divinatory arts were much esteemed in the Classical world, and were highly influential in the establishment of similar practices among the Greeks and the Romans. It is only since the decipherment of the cuneiform languages that the extent of the Classical world's debt to ancient Babylonia has become fully clear in these as in other branches of knowledge.

The study of the movements of celestial bodies was an important component of the methods used by practitioners of divination in predicting future events and interpreting the will of the gods. Yet the modern connotations of the term 'astrology', now associated with the hokum of fortune-tellers and 'your stars today' columns in newspapers and magazines, are far removed from the serious, scientific nature of this field of study in its Babylonian context. Astrology and astronomy were closely related in the Babylonian world. In fact the study of the latter could be said to have developed out of the former. For both involved detailed, systematic recording of celestial phenomena over a long period of time. Regular observations of the movements of the stars and planets, carried out for the purpose of predicting the future or interpreting the divine will, led to the realization that the movements of these celestial bodies, and phenomena such as eclipses, could be predicted, with the aid of mathematical calculations, and recognized as natural recurring phenomena rather than as random events caused by the whims of divine beings.

The study of astronomy in Babylonia goes back at least to the first half of the second millennium BC, when we learn that observations were recorded of the planet Venus's movements during the reign of Ammi-saduqa (c.1646–1626), the second-to-last member of Hammurabi's dynasty. The recording of celestial omens continued from this time onwards, if not also before, and was used as one of the main bases for developing a Babylonian calendrical system. In the mid-eighth century, during the reign of Nabonassar, accurate lists of eclipses were made, and by the end of the century both lunar and the much less frequent solar eclipses could be predicted with a fairly high degree of accuracy. By the middle of the first millennium, the study of astronomy was being established on a firm scientific basis. Even so, it remained closely linked with the art of prognostication, and those who practised astronomy for the purpose of interpreting the divine will maintained a place among the most distinguished scholars in Babylonian society.

The zodiac was invented late in the first millennium BC, and with that came the development of personal horoscopy, in which an individual's future was mapped out by an 'expert' in reading what the stars foretold for that person. But this seems not to have been a serious occupation of genuine practitioners of the astrological arts, though the casting of personal horoscopes apparently gained in fashion from the first century BC onwards.

With the fall of the Neo-Babylonian empire to Persia in 539, the reputation acquired by the practitioners of the arts of divination, including the interpretation of the will of the gods through the observation and interpretation of celestial phenomena, continued to be highly esteemed in the Classical world. The name 'Chaldaean' (used as a synonym for 'Babylonian') was regularly applied to such practitioners, as well as to Babylonian soothsayers and diviners in general. (Alternatively, persons who actually *were* of Chaldaean origin were especially renowned in these professions.) The Hellenistic period in particular, when the Seleucid dynasty held sway over Babylonia as well as other parts of the Near Eastern world, saw the study of astronomy reach its peak as a sophisticated, mathematically based science. To this period belongs the greatest of the Babylonian astronomers, Kidinnu, who practised his profession in the second half of the fourth century BC. Already by then, and increasingly so thereafter, Babylonian and Greek astronomers began to work in partnership. More generally, as Joan Oates comments: 'Astrology as well as maths and astronomy was much developed and later expanded in the Classical world, and Hellenistic science—later transmitted through Arab sources—was to dominate the ancient world and western Europe till the time of Newton. But its roots lay in Babylonia, and the Babylonian astronomy of Seleucid times, with over a millennium of remarkable mathematical development behind it, was without question a major force in the development of true science in the ancient world.'

Yet the image of Babylon as the archetypal city of decadence, profligacy, and unrestrained vice is the one that remains paramount in modern perceptions. Thanks to the influence of the

Judaeo-Christian view of Babylon, strongly reinforced by the lurid depictions of the city and its rulers in western art, this image continues to dominate all others, despite all that modern Mesopotamian scholars have done to provide a more balanced view of this, the centre of one of the world's greatest civilizations.

Chronology of major events, periods, and rulers

(All dates prior to the Neo-Babylonian period are approximate. Both higher and lower sets of dates have been proposed by various scholars for the Bronze and Iron Ages.)

Early Bronze Age

2900–2334	The Early Dynastic period
2234–2193	The Akadian Empire
2112–2004	The Ur III Empire

Middle and Late Bronze Ages

2000–1735	Old Assyrian period
1880–1595	Old Babylonian period
1792–1750	Reign of Hammurabi
early C17–early C12	Hittite Kingdom
1595	Hittite destruction of Babylon
–1570–1155	Kassite dynasty

Iron Age

1154–1027	Second dynasty of Isin
1026–1006	Second Sealand dynasty
1005–986	Bazi dynasty
979–732	'Dynasty of E'
911–610	Neo-Assyrian empire

Neo-Babylonian period (reigns dated from first full regnal year)

626–539	Neo-Babylonian empire
625–605	Reign of Nabopolassar
604–562	Reign of Nebuchadnezzar
587 or 586	Destruction of Jerusalem
555–539	Reign of Nabonidus

Persian period

559–330	Persian empire
559–530	Reign of Cyrus II
539	Cyrus captures Babylon
330	Babylonia falls to Alexander

Hellenistic and Roman periods

323	Alexander dies in Babylon
305–64	Seleucid empire
247 BC–AD 224	Parthian empire
late C1 BC–AD C2/3	Babylonia and Rome

Kinglists (main Babylonian periods; reigns dated from first full regnal year)

Old Babylonian kings (approximate dates)

(Sumu-abum)	1894–1881
Sumu-la-El	1880–1845
Sabium	1844–1831
Apil-Sin	1830–1813
Sin-muballit	1812–1793
Hammurabi	1792–1750
Samsu-iluna	1749–1712
Abi-eshuh	1711–1684
Ammi-ditana	1683–1647
Ammi-saduqa	1646–1626
Samsu-ditana	1625–1595

Kassite kings (approximate dates)

Agum II	–1570–
Burnaburiash I	–1530–
Kashtiliash III	late C16
Ulamburiash	–1500–
three kings	early–late C15
Kurigalzu I	late C15–1374
Kadashman-Enlil I	1374–1360
Burnaburiash II	1359–1333
Kara-hardash	1333
Nazi-Bugash	1333
Kurigalzu II	1332–1308
Nazi-Maruttash	1307–1282

Kadashman-Turgu	1281–1264
Kadashman-Enlil II	1263–1255
Kudur-Enlil	1254–1246
Shagarakti-Shuriash	1245–1233
Kashtiliash IV	1232–1225
Enlil-nadin-shumi	1224
Kadashman-Harbe II	1223
Adad-shuma-iddin	1222–1217
Adad-shuma-usur	1216–1187
Meli-shipak	1186–1172
Marduk-apla-iddina	1171–1159
Zababa-shuma-iddina	1158
Enlil-nadin-ahi	1157–1155

Neo-Babylonian Kings

Nabopolassar	625–605
Nebuchadnezzar	604–562
Amel-Marduk	561–560
Neriglissar	559–556
Labashi-Marduk	556
Nabonidus	555–539

Babylonia

References

(Asterisks indicate publications of ancient sources in translation.)

General works on the Ancient Near East

*Bible. The New International Version is used here.

Bryce, T. R. (2009/12), *The Routledge Handbook of the Peoples and Places of Ancient Western Asia: From the Early Bronze Age to the Fall of the Persian Empire*, Abingdon: Routledge.

Bryce. T. R. and Birkett-Rees, J. (2016), *Atlas of the Ancient Near East*, Abingdon: Routledge.

*Chavalas, M. W. (ed.) (2006), *The Ancient Near East: Historical Sources in Translation*, Oxford: Blackwell.

*Hallo, W. W. and Younger, K. L. (2003), *The Context of Scripture* (3 vols.), Leiden and Boston: Brill.

Kuhrt, A. (1995), *The Ancient Near East, c. 3000–330 BC* (2 vols.), London: Routledge.

Mieroop, M. Van De (2016), *A History of the Ancient Near East*, Oxford: Wiley-Blackwell, 3rd edn.

Podany, A. H. (2013), *The Ancient Near East: A Very Short Introduction*, Oxford and New York: Oxford University Press.

Potts, D. (2012), *A Companion to the Archaeology of the Ancient Near East* (2 vols.), Oxford: Wiley-Blackwell.

*Pritchard, J. B. (ed.) (1969), *Ancient Near Eastern Texts relating to the Old Testament*, Princeton: Princeton University Press, 3rd edn.

Radner, K. and Robson, E. (eds) (2011), *The Oxford Handbook of Cuneiform Culture*, Oxford: Oxford University Press.

Roaf, M. (1996), *Cultural Atlas of Mesopotamia and the Ancient Near East*, Abingdon: Andromeda.

Sasson, J. M. (ed.) (1995a), *Civilizations of the Ancient Near East* (4 vols.), New York: Charles Scribner's Sons.

General works on Babylonia

Arnold, B. T. (2004), *Who Were the Babylonians?*, Atlanta: Society of Biblical Literature.

Galter, H. D. (2007), 'Looking Down the Tigris', in G. Leick (ed.), 527–40.

Gill, A. (2011), *The Rise and Fall of Babylon*, London: Quercus.

*Glassner, J.-J. (2004), *Mesopotamian Chronicles*, Atlanta: Society of Biblical Literature.

Leick, G. (2003), *The Babylonians*, London and New York: Routledge.

Leick, G. (ed.) (2007), *The Babylonian World*, London and New York: Routledge.

Oates, J. (1986), *Babylon*, London: Thames and Hudson, rev. edn.

Saggs, H. W. F. (2000), *Babylonians*, Berkeley and Los Angeles: University of California Press.

Sallaberger, W. (2007), 'The Palace and the Temple in Babylonia', in G. Leick (ed.), 265–75.

Steele, L. D. (2007), 'Women and Gender in Babylonia', in G. Leick (ed.), 299–316.

Chapter 1: The Old Babylonian period

Arnold, B. T. (2004), *Who Were the Babylonians?*, Atlanta: Society of Biblical Literature, 35–60.

Charpin, D. (2012), *Hammurabi of Babylon*, London and New York: I.B.Tauris.

Charpin, D. (2015), *Gods, Kings, and Merchants in Old Babylonian Mesopotamia*, Leuven: Peeters.

Heinz, M. (2012), 'The Ur III, Old Babylonian, and Kassite Empires', in D. Potts (ed.), 713–16 (whole chapter, 706–21).

Kuhrt, A. (1995), *The Ancient Near East, c. 3000–330 BC*, London: Routledge, 108–17.

Mieroop, M. Van De (2005), *King Hammurabi of Babylon*, Oxford: Blackwell.

Sasson, J. M. (1995b), 'King Hammurabi of Babylon', in J. M. Sasson (ed.) (1995a), 901–15.

*Sasson, J. M. (2015), *From the Mari Archives: An Anthology of Old Babylonian Letters*, Winona Lake: Eisenbrauns.

Chapter 2: Babylonian society through the perspective of Hammurabi's Laws

Epigraph from the Epilogue of the Laws of Hammurabi, inspired by the translation of Martha Roth, 1997: 133–4.

*Charpin, D. (2000), 'Lettres et procès paléo-babyloniens', in F. Joannès (ed.), *Rendre la justice en Mésopotamie*, Paris: Presses Universitaires de Vincennes, 69–111.

Dassow, E. Von (2011), 'Freedom in Ancient Near Eastern Societies', in K. Radner and E. Robson (eds), 205–24.

Koppen, F. van (2007), 'Aspects of Society and Economy in the Later Old Babylonian Period', in G. Leick (ed.), 210–23.

Mieroop, M. Van De (2016), *A History of the Ancient Near East*, Oxford: Wiley-Blackwell, 3rd edn, 118–27.

*Roth, M. T. (1997), *Law Collections from the Ancient World*, Atlanta: Society of Biblical Literature, 71–142.

*Roth, M. T. (2003), 'The Laws of Hammurabi', in W. W. Hallo and K. L. Younger Jr (eds), *The Context of Scripture*, vol. II, 335–53.

Chapter 3: Old Babylonian cities

Baker, H. D. (2011), 'From Street Altar to Palace: Reading the Built Urban Environment', in K. Radner and E. Robson (eds), 533–52.

Crawford, H. (2007), 'Architecture in the Old Babylonian Period', in G. Leick (ed.), 81–94.

Goddeeris, A. (2007), 'The Old Babylonian Economy', in G. Leick (ed.), 198–209.

Reynolds, F. (2007), 'Food and Drink in Babylonia', in G. Leick (ed.), 171–84.

Chapter 4: The Kassites

Bryce, T. R. (2007), 'A View from Hattusa', in G. Leick (ed.), 503–14.

Heinz, M. (2012), 'The Ur III, Old Babylonian, and Kassite Empires', in D. Potts (ed.), 716–20 (whole chapter, 706–21).

Kuhrt, A. (1995), *The Ancient Near East, c. 3000–330 BC*, London: Routledge, 332–48.

Mieroop, M. Van De (2016), *A History of the Ancient Near East*, Oxford: Wiley-Blackwell, 3rd edn, 183–90.

*Moran, W. L. (1992), *The Amarna Letters*, Baltimore and London: Johns Hopkins Press, 1–36.

Sommerfeld, W. (1995), 'The Kassites of Ancient Mesopotamia', in J. M. Sasson (ed.) (1995a), 917–30.

Vermaak, P. S. (2007), 'Relations between Babylonia and the Levant during the Kassite period', in G. Leick (ed.), 515–26.

Warburton, D. A. (2007), 'Egypt and Mesopotamia', in G. Leick (ed.), 487–502.

Chapter 5: Writing, scribes, and literature

*Dalley, S. (2008), *Myths from Mesopotamia: Creation, the Flood, Gilgamesh and others*, Oxford: Oxford University Press, rev. edn.

*Foster, B. R. (2005), *Before the Muses: An Anthology of Akkadian Literature*, Bethesda: CDL Press, 3rd edn.

*George, A. R. (1999), *The Epic of Gilgamesh: A New Translation*, London: Penguin.

*George, A. R. (2003), *The Babylonian Gilgamesh Epic: Introduction, Critical Edition and Cuneiform Texts*, Oxford: Oxford University Press.

Koch, U. S. (2011), 'Sheep and Sky: Systems of Divinatory Interpretation', in K. Radner and E. Robson (eds), 447–69.

Koppen, F. van (2011), 'The Scribe of the Flood Story and his Circle', in K. Radner and E. Robson (eds), 140–66.

Maul, S. M. (2007), 'Divination Culture and the Handling of the Future', in G. Leick (ed.), 361–72.

Moran, W. L. (1995), 'The Gilgamesh Epic: A Masterpiece from Ancient Mesopotamia', in J. M. Sasson (ed.) (1995a), 2327–36.

Rochberg, F. (2011), 'Observing and Describing the World through Divination and Astronomy', in K. Radner and E. Robson (eds), 618–36.

*Sandars, N. (1971), *Poems of Heaven and Hell from Ancient Mesopotamia*, London: Penguin.

Veldhuis, N. (2011), 'Levels of Literacy', in K. Radner and E. Robson (eds), 68–89.

Wasserman, N. (2003), *Style and Form in Old-Babylonian Literary Texts*, Cuneiform Monographs 27, Leiden: Brill.

Chapter 6: The long interlude

Arnold, B. T. (2004), *Who Were the Babylonians?*, Atlanta: Society of Biblical Literature, 75–85.

Babylonia

Brinkman, J. A. (1982), 'Babylonia c. 1000–748 B.C.', *Cambridge Ancient History* III.1, 282–313.

Brinkman, J. A. (1991), 'Babylonia in the Shadow of Assyria (747–626 B.C.)', *Cambridge Ancient History* III.2, 1–70.

Frame, G. (1992), *Babylonia 689–627 B. C.: A Political History*, Leiden: NINO.

*Frame, G. (1995), *Rulers of Babylonia: From the Second Dynasty of Isin to the End of Assyrian Domination (1157–612 BC)*, Toronto, Buffalo, and London: University of Toronto.

*Glassner, J.-J. (2004), *Mesopotamian Chronicles*, Atlanta: Society of Biblical Literature, 193–211.

Jursa, M. (2007), 'The Babylonian Economy in the First Millennium BC', in G. Leick (ed.), 224–35.

Jursa, M. (2010), *Aspects of the Economic History of Babylonia in the First Millennium BC: Economic Geography, Economic Mentalities, Agriculture, the Use of Money and the Problem of Economic Growth*, Münster: Ugarit Verlag.

Kuhrt, A. (1995), *The Ancient Near East, c. 3000–330 BC*, London: Routledge, 573–89.

Oates, J. (1986), *Babylon*, London: Thames and Hudson, rev. edn, 104–14.

Chapter 7: The Neo-Babylonian empire

Arnold, B. T. (2004), *Who Were the Babylonians?*, Atlanta: Society of Biblical Literature, 87–105.

*Arnold, B. T. and Michalowski, P. (2006), 'Achaemenid Period Historical Texts concerning Mesopotamia', in M. W. Chavalas (ed.), 407–26.

Baker, H. D. (2007), 'Urban Form in the First Millennium B.C.', in G. Leick (2007), 66–77.

Baker, H. D. (2012), 'The Neo-Babylonian Empire', in D. Potts (ed.), 914–30.

Beaulieu, P.-A. (1989), *The Reign of Nabonidus, King of Babylon 556–539 B.C.*, Yale Near Eastern Researches 10. New Haven: Yale University Press.

Beaulieu, P.-A. (1995), 'King Nabonidus and the Neo-Babylonian Empire', in J. M. Sasson (ed.) (1995a), 969–79.

Beaulieu, P.-A. (2007), 'Nabonidus the Mad King', in M. Heinz and M. H. Feldman (eds), *Representations of Political Power: Case Histories from Times of Change and Dissolving Order in the Ancient Near East*, Winona Lake: Eisenbrauns, 137–66.

*Glassner, J.-J. (2004), *Mesopotamian Chronicles*, Atlanta: Society of Biblical Literature, 214–39.

Jursa, M. (2005), *Neo-Babylonian Legal and Administrative Documents: Typology, Contents and Archives*, Guides to the Mesopotamian Textual Record 1, Münster: Ugarit-Verlag.

Jursa, M. (2007), 'Die Söhne Kudurrus und die Herkunft der neubabylonischen Dynastie', *Revue d'assyrologie et d'archéologie orientale* 101: 125–36.

Jursa, M. (2010), *Aspects of the Economic History of Babylonia in the First Millennium BC: Economic Geography, Economic Mentalities, Agriculture, the Use of Money and the Problem of Economic Growth*, Münster: Ugarit Verlag.

Jursa, M. (2014), 'The Neo-Babylonian Empire', in M. Gehler and R. Rollinger (eds), *Imperien und Reiche in der Weltgeschichte-Epochübergreifenden und globalhistorische Vergleiche*, Wiesbaden: Harrassowitz, 121–48.

Mieroop, M. Van De (2009), 'The Empires of Assyria and Babylonia', in T. Harrison (ed.), *The Great Empires of the Ancient World*, London: Thames & Hudson, 70–97.

Mieroop, M. Van De (2016), *A History of the Ancient Near East*, Oxford: Wiley-Blackwell, 3rd edn, 294–307.

*Pearce, L. E. and Wunsch, C. (2014), *Documents of Judean Exiles and West Semites in Babylonia in the Collection of David Sofer*, Cornell University Studies in Assyriology and Sumerology 28, Bethesda, MD: CDL Press.

Roaf, M. (1996), *Cultural Atlas of Mesopotamia and the Ancient Near East*, Abingdon: Andromeda, 198–202.

*Roth, M. T. (1997), *Law Collections from the Ancient World*, Atlanta: Scholars Press, 143–9.

*Studevent-Hickman, B., Melville, S. C., and Noegel, S. (2006), 'Neo-Babylonian Period Texts from Babylonia and Syro-Palestine', in M. W. Chavalas (ed.), 382–406.

Waerzeggers, C. (2011), 'The Pious King: Royal Patronage of Temples', in K. Radner and E. Robson (eds), 725–51.

Wiseman, D. J. (1991), 'Babylonia 605–539 B.C.', *Cambridge Ancient History* III.2, 229–51.

Chapter 8: Nebuchadnezzar's Babylon

Baker, H. D. (2011), 'From Street Altar to Palace: Reading the Built Urban Environment', in K. Radner and E. Robson (eds), 533–52.

Dalley, S. (2013), *The Mystery of the Hanging Gardens of Babylon*, Oxford: Oxford University Press.

Finkel, I. L. and Seymour, M. J. (eds) (2008), *Babylon: Myth and Reality*, London: British Museum Press.

Mieroop, M. Van De (2003), 'Reading Babylon', *American Journal of Archaeology* 107: 257–75.

Chapter 9: Babylonia in later ages

Aaboe, A. (1980), 'Observation and Theory in Babylonian Astronomy', *Centaurus* 24: 14–35.

Aaboe, A. (1991), 'Babylonian Mathematics, Astrology, and Astronomy', *Cambridge Ancient History*, III.2, 276–92.

Boiy, T. (2004), *Late Achaemenid and Hellenistic Babylon*, Orientalia Lovaniensia Analecta 136, Leuven: Peeters.

Breucker, G. de (2011), 'Berossos between Transition and Innovation', in K. Radner and E. Robson (eds), 637–57.

Brown, D. (2008), 'Increasingly Redundant: The Growing Obsolescence of the Cuneiform Script in Babylonia from 539 BC,' in J. Baines, J. Bennett, and S. Houston (eds), *The Disappearance of Writing Systems: Perspectives in Literacy and Communication*, London: Equinox: 73–102.

Chambon, G. (2011), 'Numeracy and Metrology', in K. Radner and E. Robson (eds), 51–67.

Clancier, P. (2011), 'Cuneiform Culture's Last Guardians: The Old Urban Notability of Hellenistic Uruk', in K. Radner and E. Robson (eds), 753–73.

*Glassner, J.-J. (2004), *Mesopotamian Chronicles*, Atlanta: Society of Biblical Literature, 240–58.

Kuhrt, A. (2007), 'The Persian Empire', in G. Leick (ed.), 562–76.

Robson, E. (2007), 'Mathematics, Metrology, and Professional Numeracy', in G. Leick (ed.), 418–31.

Rochberg, F. (2011), 'Observing and Describing the World through Divination and Astronomy', in K. Radner and E. Robson (eds), 618–36.

Spek, R. J. van de (1985), 'The Babylonian Temple during the Macedonian and Parthian domination, *Bibliotheca Orientalis* 42: 541–62.

Spek, R. J. van de (2006), 'The Size and Significance of the Babylonian Temples under the Successors', in P. Briant and F. Joannès (eds), *La transition entre l'empire achéménide et les royaumes hellenistiques*, Paris: De Boccard, 261–307.

Waerzeggers, C. (2003/4), 'The Babylonian Revolts against Xerxes and the "End Archives"', *Archiv für Orientforschung* 50: 150–78.

Further reading

For full details of the following publications see the References section under the relevant chapter headings.

Comprehensive works on the ancient Near East, which provide a broad context for the study of Babylonia, include Kuhrt (1995), *The Ancient Near East, c. 3000–330 BC*, Van De Mieroop (2016), *A History of the Ancient Near East* (up to date, and more accessible for general readers), Podany (2013), *The Ancient Near East: A Very Short Introduction* (concise and selective in its treatment, but including brief chapters on the main periods of Babylonian history), and Sasson (1995a), *Civilizations of the Ancient Near East* (4-volume encyclopaedic work with contributions by many scholars). Bryce (2009/12), *The Routledge Handbook of the Peoples and Places of Ancient Western Asia*, provides an encyclopaedia-type coverage of Near Eastern peoples, cities, and kingdoms. Chavalas (2006), *The Ancient Near East*, provides translations, with introductory notes, of a wide range of written records of the ancient Near East.

General works on Babylon and Babylonia include Arnold (2004), *Who Were the Babylonians?* (catering both for students and general readers), Gill (2011), *The Rise and Fall of Babylon* (copiously illustrated, written for a very general audience, and briefly covering other contemporary Near Eastern civilizations as well), Leick (2003), *The Babylonians* (a concise account of Babylonian history and civilization), Leick (2007), *The Babylonian World* (chapters by individual scholars on numerous aspects of Babylonian history and civilization), Oates (1986), *Babylon* (inevitably dated but highly readable, with coverage of Babylonian history down to the Hellenistic period), and Saggs (2000), *Babylonians* (with some updating of earlier editions).

There are a number of scholarly chapters relevant to Babylonian society and culture in Radner and Robson (2011), *The Oxford Handbook of Cuneiform Culture*. On the two institutions which dominated Babylonian life, the palace and the temple, see Sallaberger (2007), 'The Palace and the Temple in Babylonia'. On the roles, activities, and status of women in Babylonian society, see Steele (2007), 'Women and Gender in Babylonia', and for an account of what the Babylonians ate and drank, Reynolds (2007), 'Food and Drink in Babylonia'. Galter (2007), 'Looking Down the Tigris', discusses political, military, and cultural relations between Babylonia and Assyria to the end of the Neo-Assyrian empire (late seventh century BC).

Accounts of the first major period of Babylonian history, the Old Babylonian Kingdom (Chapters 1–3), naturally focus on the kingdom's defining figure, Hammurabi. These accounts include books by Charpin (2012), *Hammurabi of Babylon* and Van De Mieroop (2005), *King Hammurabi of Babylon* (both highly authoritative, though with different emphases and approaches), and a chapter by Sasson (1995b), 'King Hammurabi of Babylon'. Roth (1997: 71–142), *Law Collections from the Ancient World* (1997: 71–142) and (2003), 'The Laws of Hammurabi', provides one of the most recent translations of Hammurabi's Laws. Charpin (2000), 'Lettres et procès paléo-babyloniens' and (2012: Chapters 8–10), *Hammurabi of Babylon*, provides references to and translations of a number of legal and administrative documents and letters dating to Hammurabi's reign; these contain much information about the system of justice and its management in this period. See also Sasson (2015), *From the Mari Archives: An Anthology of Old Babylonian Letters*. Von Dassow (2011), 'Freedom in Ancient Near Eastern Societies' provides important information on Babylonian social classes as reflected in Hammurabi's Laws. Goddeeris (2007), 'The Old Babylonian Economy', gives an account of the Old Babylonian economy, and van Koppen (2007), 'Aspects of Society and Economy in the Later Old Babylonian Period', discusses both social and economic aspects of the period. Crawford (2007), 'Architecture in the Old Babylonian Period', provides an account of Old Babylonian architecture—public buildings, palaces, temples, and domestic housing.

The Kassite period of Babylonian history (Chapter 4) is covered at some length in all general works on Babylonia. In addition, see Kuhrt (1995: 344–8), *The Ancient Near East*, and Sommerfeld (1995), 'The Kassites of Ancient Mesopotamia'. For translations of relevant documents from the period, see W. Moran (1992: 1–37), *The Amarna Letters*, and Chavalas (2006: 275–9), *The Ancient Near East: Historical Sources in Translation*. For Kassite Babylonia's relations with Egypt, see Warburton (2007), 'Egypt and Mesopotamia', with Hatti (the Hittite kingdom), see Bryce (2007), 'A View from Hattusa', and with the Levant, Vermaak (2007), 'Relations between Babylonia and the Levant during the Kassite period'.

Several 'classics' of Babylonian literature are discussed in Chapter 5. For an overview of the Gilgamesh epic, see Moran (1995), 'The Gilgamesh Epic: A Masterpiece from Ancient Mesopotamia'. George (1999), *The Epic of Gilgamesh: A New Translation*, translates and discusses the epic, and in (2003), *The Babylonian Gilgamesh Epic: Introduction, Critical Edition and Cuneiform Texts*, provides a scholarly edition of it. For translations of other Mesopotamian epics and myths, see Sandars (1971), *Poems of Heaven and Hell from Ancient Mesopotamia*, Hallo and Younger (2003: vol. I, 449–60), *The Context of Scripture*, Dalley (2008), *Myths from Mesopotamia: Creation, the Flood, Gilgamesh and others*. Van Koppen (2011), 'The Scribe of the Flood Story and his Circle', discusses the Atram-Hasis epic, its origins and authorship. For an introduction to Old Babylonian Akkadian inscriptions, see Wasserman (2003), *Style and Form in Old-Babylonian Literary Texts*. See also *Sources of Early Akkadian Literature*, a continuing Leipzig University Project, online at www.seal.uni-leipzig.de. Veldhuis (2011), 'Levels of Literacy', discusses the extent of literacy in Babylonian society. On divinatory practices, see Maul (2007), 'Divination Culture and the Handling of the Future'.

The interlude between the Kassite and Neo-Babylonian periods (Chapter 6) is covered in greater or lesser detail by all the above-mentioned general works on Babylonia. Brinkman (1982), 'Babylonia c. 1000–748 B.C.', and (1991) 'Babylonia in the Shadow of Assyria (747–626 B.C.)', provide detailed (though now somewhat dated) accounts of the period. Written sources for the period are translated in Frame (1995), *Rulers of Babylonia: From the Second Dynasty of Isin to the End of Assyrian Domination*, and (from Nabonassar's reign to 668 BC) Glassner (2004: 193–211),

Mesopotamian Chronicles. On the history of the Babylonian economy in the first millennium BC (including the Neo-Babylonian period), see Jursa (2007a), 'The Babylonian Economy in the First Millennium BC' and (2010), *Aspects of the Economic History of Babylonia in the First Millennium BC*.

In addition to treatments of the Neo-Babylonian period (Chapters 7–8) in the general works on Babylonia, see also Wiseman (1991), 'Babylonia 605–539 B.C.' (now obviously dated), Baker (2007), 'Urban Form in the First Millennium B.C.', and (2011), 'From Street Altar to Palace: Reading the Built Urban Environment' (on the layout of the Neo-Babylonian cities, the latter from the viewpoint of the ordinary inhabitants of the Babylonian cities). For comprehensive, up-to-date accounts of the Neo-Babylonian empire in general, see Baker (2012), 'The Neo-Babylonian Empire' and Jursa (2014), 'The Neo-Babylonian Empire'. On Nabonidus's reign, see Beaulieu (1989), *The Reign of Nabonidus, King of Babylon 556–539 BC*, (1995), 'King Nabonidus and the Neo-Babylonian Empire', and (2007), 'Nabonidus the Mad King'. On the Hanging Gardens and other aspects of the Neo-Babylonian period, including references to and translations of the relevant Classical sources, see Dalley (2013), *The Mystery of the Hanging Gardens of Babylon*. Jursa (2007), 'Die Söhne Kudurrus und die Herkunft der neubabylonischen Dynastie', discusses the origins of the Neo-Babylonian dynasty. Van De Mieroop (2003), 'Reading Babylon', provides an account of the ideologies underlying the built environment of Nebuchadnezzar's Babylon, and in (2009), 'The Empires of Assyria and Babylonia', a lavishly illustrated overview of both the Neo-Assyrian and Neo-Babylonian empires.

The Book of Daniel is the *locus classicus* for the biblical account of Nebuchadnezzar's and (allegedly) Belshazzar's reigns. For translations of Babylonian records of the period, see Glassner (2004: 214–39), *Mesopotamian Chronicles*, Studevent-Hickman *et al.* (2006), 'Neo-Babylonian Period Texts from Babylonia and Syro-Palestine', and Roth (1997: 143–9), *Law Collections from the Ancient World* (translation of the Neo-Babylonian Laws). Adad-guppi's biography is translated by J. A. Wilson in Pritchard (1969: 560–2), *Ancient Near Eastern Texts relating to the Old Testament*, and by S. C. Melville in Chavalas (2006: 389–93), *The Ancient Near East: Historical Sources in Translation*. The so-called 'Nabonidus Chronicle', an account of her son's reign and the Persian conquest of his kingdom, is translated by B. T. Arnold and

P. Michalowski in Chavalas (2006: 418–20), and the 'Verse
Account of Nabonidus' by A. L. Oppenheim in Pritchard (1969:
312–15). The 'Chronicle' and 'Verse Account' both reflect strong
pro-Persian, anti-Nabonidus bias.

Jursa (2005), *Neo-Babylonian Legal and Administrative Documents*,
provides a survey of currently known legal and administrative
documents dating from the Neo-Babylonian to the Parthian
period, and Pearce and Wunsch (2014), *Documents of Judean
Exiles and West Semites in Babylonia in the Collection of David
Sofer*, deal with texts relating to the settlement of Jewish deportees
in the Babylonian countryside. Waerzeggers (2011), 'The Pious
King: Royal Patronage of Temples', discusses the ideology of
kingship, with particular reference to the king's role in the religious
activities of Babylonian society. Finkel and Seymour (2008),
Babylon: Myth and Reality (Catalogue of a British Museum
exhibition), is a lavishly illustrated treatment of many aspects of
Babylon's history and civilization during the Neo-Babylonian
period.

For brief accounts of Babylonia under Persian, Macedonian, Seleucid,
Parthian, and Roman rule (Chapter 9), see Oates (1986: 136–44),
Babylon, and Leick (2003: 61–9), *The Babylonians*. Kuhrt (2007),
'The Persian Empire', provides an overview of the Persian empire
and Babylonia's place within it. Waerzeggers (2003/4), 'The
Babylonian Revolts against Xerxes and the "End Archives"',
analyses the Borsippa archives and the bearing they have on the
dates of the uprisings against Xerxes. For translated passages from
the Babylonian Chronicles of these periods, see Glassner (2004:
240–56), *Mesopotamian Chronicles*, and Chavalas (2006:
407–26), *The Ancient Near East: Historical Sources in Translation*.
The Cyrus Cylinder inscription is translated by P. Michalowski in
Chavalas (2006: 426–30). Clancier (2011), 'Cuneiform Culture's
Last Guardians: The Old Urban Notability of Hellenistic Uruk',
provides an account of the survival of the cuneiform culture in
Babylonia during the Hellenistic period, and de Breucker (2011),
'Berossos between Transition and Innovation', an account of the
Babylonian scholar Berossos's contribution to both Babylonian and
Greek scholarship in the Hellenistic period.

For the decline and disappearance of the cuneiform writing system,
see Brown (2008), 'Increasingly Redundant: The Growing
Obsolescence of the Cuneiform Script in Babylonia from 539 BC'.
On the role of the Babylonian temple in post-Neo-Babylonian

periods, see van der Spek (1985), 'The Babylonian Temple during the Macedonian and Parthian Domination', and (2006), 'The Size and Significance of the Babylonian Temples under the Successors'. On Babylon itself in the late Persian and Hellenistic periods, see Boiy (2004), *Late Achaemenid and Hellenistic Babylon*. Further on the legacy of Babylon (Chapter 9), see Oates (1986: 163–98), *Babylon*, and Finkel and Seymour (2008: 166–212), *Babylon: Myth and Reality*.

For accounts of mathematics and metrology in Babylonia and elsewhere in the ancient Near East (end of Chapter 9), see Aaboe (1991), 'Babylonian Mathematics, Astrology, and Astronomy', Robson (2007), 'Mathematics, Metrology, and Professional Numeracy', and Chambon (2011), 'Numeracy and Metrology'. On the observation and recording of celestial phenomena, see Aaboe (1980), 'Observation and Theory in Babylonian Astronomy', and (1991), 'Babylonian Mathematics, Astrology, and Astronomy', and also Koch (2011), 'Sheep and Sky: Systems of Divinatory Interpretation', and Rochberg (2011), 'Observing and Describing the World through Divination and Astronomy'.

Index

Index

ALEXANDER THE GREAT
A Very Short Introduction
Hugh Bowden

Alexander the Great became king of Macedon in 336 BC, when he was only 20 years old, and died at the age of 32, twelve years later. But what do we really know about Alexander? In this *Very Short Introduction*, Hugh Bowden goes behind the usual historical accounts of Alexander's life and career. Instead, he focuses on the evidence from Alexander's own time—letters from officials in Afghanistan, Babylonian diaries, records from Egyptian temples—to try and understand how Alexander appeared to those who encountered him. In doing so he also demonstrates the profound influence the legends of his life have had on our historical understanding and the controversy they continue to generate worldwide.

"Bowden covers all the highlights of Alexander's career"

Steve Craggs, Northern Echo

"It's an interesting read for those who do know something of Alexander, as well as for initiates"

Adrian Spooner, Classics for All

ANCIENT ASSYRIA
A Very Short Introduction
Karen Radner

Assyria was one of the most influential kingdoms of the Ancient
Near East. In this *Very Short Introduction*, Karen Radner sketches
the history of Assyria from city state to empire, from the early
2nd millennium BC to the end of the 7th century BC. Since the
archaeological rediscovery of Assyria in the mid-19th century, its
cities have been excavated extensively in Iraq, Syria, Turkey and
Israel, with further sites in Iran, Lebanon, and Jordan providing
important information. The Assyrian Empire was one of the most
geographically vast, socially diverse, multicultural, and multi-ethnic
states of the early first millennium BC. Using archaeological
records, Radner provides insights into the lives of the inhabitants
of the kingdom, highlighting the diversity of human experiences
in the Assyrian Empire.

'The ideas and the analyses are combined in a highly
readable way, making this "pocket-sized" book a perfect
source for the non-professional reader who is interested in
one subject or another and wants to become familiar
quickly with a certain subject.'

**Journal of Ancient History and
Archaeology, Horatiu Cocis**

THE ANCIENT NEAR EAST

A Very Short Introduction

Amanda H. Podany

The Ancient Near East is known as the 'cradle of civilization' for a good reason. This *Very Short Introduction* offers a fascinating account of this momentous time in human history. Covering a period of incredible innovation from around 3500 BCE, with the founding of the first Mesopotamian cities, to the conquest of the Near East by the Persian king Cyrus the Great in 539 BCE, historian Amanda Podany overturns the popular image of the ancient world as a primitive, violent place. We discover that it was a time and place of earth-shaking changes for humankind: the beginnings of writing and law, kingship and bureaucracy, diplomacy and state-sponsored warfare, mathematics and literature.

"The book is a short, comprehensive and accessible way to first get in touch with a new subject."

Bibliotheca Orientalis